Super Natural Family

INTERNATIONAL

a Healthy and Playful Global Recipe Collection

COOKBOOK

Nancy Mehagian

Illustrations by Yoko Matsuoka

Book written by Nancy Mehagian
Illustrations: Yoko Matsuoka
Art Direction: Judith A. Proffer
design: designSimple

Published by IPG
814 North Franklin Street
Chicago, Illinois 60610
ISBN 978-1-957317-29-8
Printed in the United States of America

For my mother,
Florence Mardian Mehagian,
who blessed me with her cooking genes —
and to all the wonderful chefs and home cooks
I've met in my travels, as well as to
all the future chefs to come.

Contents

Introduction

Cooking and eating food from countries we've never visited teaches us so much about other cultures—their climates, their customs and holidays, what they grow and how they cook. It's a great way to understand how much we have in common and to honor how much we differ. So many different countries seem to have their own versions of meatballs, pancakes, and stuffed and rolled-up things and I have learned to love them all.

If you have been lucky to visit some of the 195 countries in the world today, I hope you will discover the joy of cooking some of the things in your family's kitchen that you were introduced to during your travels. Certain smells can take you right back to a special place.

Years ago I opened the first vegetarian restaurant on the island of Ibiza in Spain. That island had the most beautiful fruits and vegetables, fresh cheeses and seafood. I'm not a strict vegetarian anymore but I love creating recipes and eating healthy and natural versions of dishes whenever possible. That's where the "super natural" comes in. Natural foods really do taste better, and are so much better for us.

I had so much fun putting this cookbook together for you. Friends and family enjoyed my experiments and were always willing testers. It helps to get the whole family involved in food preparation. I love teamwork! Some recipes will be short and easy-peasy and others might have more steps and take a bit longer. It will always be worth the effort and if it doesn't come out perfectly (there's no such thing as perfect), I'm sure it will still taste great.

The recipes in this book by no means represent every country, nor all of their wonderful foods. I selected and created them because they offer an introduction to the diversity of food around the globe and because they are delicious. They also offer fun family adventures in the kitchen. No passport required.

Enjoy Your Meal!
Bon Appetit!
Guten Appetit!
Buon Appetito!
Bil Hana Wish Shifa'
Sihk Faahn!
Smakelijk Eten

Nancy

The Well-Stocked Pantry

Shopping like a chef or cook means visiting markets to see what looks especially fresh or interesting. And all experienced chefs and cooks know how important it is to have a pantry filled with the everyday essentials you'll see on this list. It makes life easier and cuts down on the time it takes to whip up a meal, bake something special or simply prepare a snack.

OILS: olive oil, sunflower oil, peanut oil, toasted sesame oil, grapeseed oil

VINEGARS: red wine vinegar, balsamic vinegar, rice vinegar

PASTA AND NOODLES: all kinds, including spaghetti, shells, elbow macaroni, rigatoni

BAKING NEEDS: whole-wheat flour, white whole-wheat flour, baking powder, baking soda, raw sugar, brown sugar, coconut sugar, vanilla extract

GRAINS: brown rice, basmati rice, jasmine rice, kasha, quinoa, rolled oats, millet, cornmeal, whole-wheat couscous

NUTS AND SEEDS: pecans, walnuts, almonds, pine nuts, sesame seeds, pumpkin seeds

HERBS AND SPICES: sea salt, black peppercorns, white pepper, curry powder, bay leaves, paprika, cinnamon, ginger, nutmeg, garlic powder, oregano, basil, thyme, rubbed sage, cumin

CANNED GOODS: evaporated milk, whole peeled tomatoes, tomato sauce, garbanzo beans, black beans, coconut milk

EXTRAS: tamari soy sauce, whole-grain mustard, Dijon mustard, fish sauce

DRIED FRUITS: raisins, currants, dried cranberries, dates

A Word on Safety

Ovens are hot and knives are sharp. Use your mitts and your wits in the kitchen, always concentrating on the task at hand. It's fun to talk and listen to music and maybe even dance a little when you're cooking, but safety must always come first. The mitts you'll see illustrated throughout the cookbook are a gentle reminder to be mindful of just that.

Besides confidence and a sense of adventure, these are some things I like to have in my kitchen to make cooking easier and more playful:

Pastry brush

Microplane

Mortar and pestle

Scraper

Silicone baking sheets

Parchment paper

Tongs

Kitchen scissors

Herbs and Spices

Julia Child famously said "the more you know, the more you can create." Salt and pepper are essentials when it comes to seasoning food (which is why you'll see some fun and fancy salt and pepper shakers as you explore these global recipes), but one of the ways to get super creative in the kitchen is to experiment with herbs and spices.

Did you know that there is medicine right on your spice rack? A tea made from *basil* leaves is good for fevers and flu. *Cardamom* warms the body and is good for tummy aches and gas. *Bay leaves* not only add a nice flavor to soups and stews but also help you digest your food.

Yogis in India believe *black pepper* to be one of Nature's most perfect spices because it helps keep them so healthy. And *cinnamon* is magic. Not only does it provide a distinct and powerful flavor we love in desserts and cereals, it also warms the whole body and is good for many different ailments, like inflammation.

My favorite spice of all has to be *ginger*. I love it in cakes and cookies. I love it with my sushi. I love it in tea when I have a sore throat and I love it in my stir-fried veggies. If you have any aches and pains, muscle cramps or nausea, use fresh ginger root. Every fridge should have some fresh ginger in it.

Ginger comes from a lily-like plant, and it is the root of the plant that is prized all over the world. This root, which can look like a stubby hand, can be used freshly grated or dried and ground into a powder. Ginger is the first authentic Asian spice to make its way to Egypt and on to ancient Greece and Rome. It is the second most highly traded spice after pepper, and today most of our ginger comes from Jamaica.

Cumin is a small seed that is a member of the parsley family. The seeds are sometimes used whole and sometimes they are ground up with a mortar and pestle. Cumin has been around a long, long time. The ancient Egyptians used it as a spice in their food—and also when they made mummies. It originally comes from the Middle East and is mostly used in Mexican, Indian, and Middle Eastern foods. Cumin is excellent in beans and fried curry dishes because it helps prevent gas. By the way, have you ever heard of "jumping beans"? My father would let me buy them when we went to Mexico. The beans don't really jump. They just move around a bit because there is a real worm inside of them. But not to worry, none of the recipes in this cookbook call for jumping beans.

The word "curry" means a richly spiced sauce, and curry powder is a combination of many different spices. Some of these spices are used whole, like the mustard seeds, and others are pounded using a mortar and pestle, like cumin, turmeric, cardamom, fennel and peppers. Many experienced cooks make their own combinations of spices. Luckily for us there are many versions of curry powder already mixed. Not all curry powders or dishes called curry are hot. Different regions like different levels of heat in their food.

I happen to like hot, spicy food. I grew up in Arizona and started eating salsa and chips when I was still in a high chair. One time in an Indian restaurant in London I ordered my curry "hot." Well, I couldn't eat it after the first bite because I had smoke coming out of my ears and my tongue felt like I'd stuck it on a hot frying pan. That's why in certain recipes I call for mild curry powder. I don't want you to explode.

Two of the herbs used the most in Mediterranean cooking are oregano and basil. Every time I smell a basil leaf it makes me think of Italy. Basil is a mild herb and there are many varieties of it since it is also used in many other countries. The word "basil" comes from the Greek language. In Greek, basil means "royal" or "kingly" and maybe that's why many chefs call it the king of herbs. The name might also come from another Greek word, "basilisk," which means a huge serpent-like lizard that can breathe on people and kill them if they look at him. There was a basilisk in *Harry Potter* that was truly scary. Maybe if we eat enough basil we can scare off the basilisk.

Oregano is an herb that is native to the hillsides of the Mediterranean region. The name "oregano" comes from the Greek language and means "joy of the mountain." It is the main flavoring in most pizza sauce and that certainly makes me full of joy.

Armenia

Armenia is where my own family is from and it was
no small task selecting the recipes to include. Fresh herbs,
dried fruit and honey are used often in Armenian cooking,
and you know I just had to include a pilaf recipe.

Nancy's Special Chicken Soup

I'm not sure how it happens, but every time I have a pot of this particular chicken soup on the stove, friends seem to turn up at my house. It's an easy soup to make and it helps that I have a lemon tree in my backyard.

6 cups chicken broth

1 large onion, chopped

3 stalks celery, diced

2 medium carrots, diced

½ cup long-grain white rice

1 cup chopped cooked chicken breast

2 eggs

Juice of 2 lemons

1 teaspoon salt

¼ teaspoon white pepper

Parsley, chopped, for garnish

Pour chicken broth into a good-sized stockpot and bring to a full boil. Add onion, celery, carrot, rice, salt, and pepper. Cover with a lid and simmer for 20 minutes. Stir in the chicken.

In a small bowl beat the eggs. Add lemon juice to the beaten eggs, along with about ¼ cup of the hot soup, then slowly add to the pot. The lemon juice "bleaches" the soup, turning it into a lovely, creamy white. Sprinkle with chopped parsley and serve. Everyone loves this soup, and how easy was that? Serves 4 to 6.

Bulghur Pilaf

Bulghur pilaf is Armenian soul food, our version of grits. It's an easy and delicious side dish and is great the next day for leftovers.

¼ cup olive oil or melted butter, or a combination of both

1 medium onion, chopped

½ green bell pepper, diced

2 medium tomatoes, chopped

2 cups bulghur (#4 size)

1 teaspoon salt

Black pepper, to taste

3½ cups boiling water, vegetable or chicken broth

Sauté onion and pepper in oil or butter. Add the tomatoes and cook until soft. Next, stir in the bulghur, salt and pepper and stir well until all the grains are coated in the oil or butter. Finally, add the boiling liquid and bring to a full boil, then reduce the heat to simmer. Cover with a lid and cook for 20 to 30 minutes or until all liquid is absorbed.

Let the bulghur stand for 10 minutes and fluff lightly with a fork before serving. Serves 6 to 8.

Rice Pilaf

This authentic version of the "San Francisco treat" in a box has been a supermarket sensation for decades, and if you ask any Armenian kid what their favorite food is they will say pilaf. Grown-ups love it too. Now you can make your own with this easy recipe.

¼ cup butter
2 to 3 rounds of vermicelli noodles
2 cups long-grain white rice
1 teaspoon salt
5 cups boiling chicken broth

Melt butter in a heavy saucepan. Break up the vermicelli with your hands and brown it in the butter, stirring constantly. You will need to keep a close eye on the pan so the butter does not burn, though it will start to get a little brown. Add the rice and salt and stir a few minutes more. Finally, stir in the boiling broth, cover pot with tight-fitting lid, and simmer on very low heat for 20 to 25 minutes or until all liquid is absorbed. Fluff rice with a spoon and let pilaf stand at least 10 minutes before serving. Serves 6 to 8.

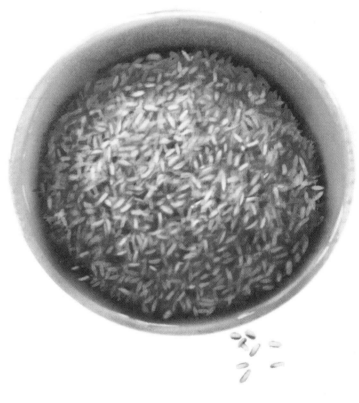

Fassoulia
(String Bean Stew)

This was my father's favorite dish to make.
Aren't food memories the best?

¼ cup olive oil

1 large onion, chopped

3 cloves garlic, minced

½ green bell pepper, chopped

3 large ripe tomatoes,
  chopped

1 pound green beans,
  washed, trimmed and
  sliced

1 teaspoon salt

½ teaspoon black pepper

In a heavy pot, sauté onion
and garlic in olive oil until
soft. Stir in the bell pepper and
continue to sauté a few minutes
longer. Next, stir in the tomatoes.
Add the green beans, salt and pepper,
stir and cover with a lid. Simmer over low
heat for 20 minutes, stirring occasionally, until
beans are tender. Serves 4 to 6.

Kataif
(Shredded Dough Pastry)

This is an old family recipe with a couple of contemporary ingredients. It's really fun to make because the shredded dough is both strange and wonderful.

You will need a 10 x 14 x 2-inch baking pan

1 cup unsalted butter

1 pound kataif dough

> ### FILLING
> **8 ounces cream cheese, softened**
>
> **1 pound small curd cottage cheese**
>
> **2 eggs, beaten**
>
> **½ cup honey**
>
> **1 teaspoon vanilla extract**

> ### SYRUP
> **½ cup honey**
>
> **1½ cups raw sugar**
>
> **1 cup water**
>
> **2 tablespoons lemon juice, strained**

Preheat oven to 375°F. In the bowl of your electric mixer, blend both cheeses, eggs, honey and vanilla together until smooth. Set aside.

Remove the kataif from the package. In a large and deep mixing bowl, begin pulling apart the shredded dough with your fingers until all the strands are loose. This is the fun part. When all the strands of dough are loose, pour melted butter, half at a time, over the dough and toss lightly with your fingers until all the dough is coated with butter. Cover the bottom of a baking pan with half the buttered dough. Next, spoon the cheese filling on top, spreading around all the dough. Then spread the remaining dough on the top.

Place tray on lower shelf of oven and bake for 10 minutes; then place on the top shelf and bake for 20 minutes longer, or until the dough is golden brown on top. Remove from oven and allow to cool.

To prepare syrup: Mix honey, sugar, water and lemon juice in a small saucepan. Stir until sugar dissolves. Bring mixture to a boil. Then lower the heat to medium and cook for 15 minutes. Allow to cool a little, then pour the syrup over the pastry and serve slightly warm. Serves 12.

Australia

Australia is a magical place, with koalas, kangaroos and even laughing kookaburras. A favorite childhood dessert there is a simple piece of white bread smeared with butter and topped with sprinkles. It's called Fairy Bread and there's really no way to prepare it super naturally, but it's something fun to know about if you ever want to have a quick taste of something from Down Under.

Anzac Biscuits
(Coconut Oat Bars)

These cookies were made by Australian and New Zealand women to send to the soldiers in World War I (the Australian/New Zealand Army Corps), which is how they got their name. They may be called biscuits, but they are a deliciously sweet coconut treat.

1 cup whole-wheat flour

¾ cup raw sugar

1 cup rolled oats

1 cup dried and flaked coconut

½ cup butter

1 tablespoon pure maple syrup

1 teaspoon baking soda

2 tablespoons hot water

Preheat oven to 350°F. In a large mixing bowl blend together the flour, sugar, oats and coconut. Set aside.

In a small saucepan, melt the butter and then stir in the syrup. Mix the baking soda and hot water together in a small bowl and pour into the butter/syrup mixture. Stir this well and watch it get foamy.

Stir the foamy mixture into the dry mixture and mix well. This will be a loose dough. Grease or spray a 9-inch baking dish and then press the biscuit mixture into the baking pan. Bake for 30 to 35 minutes or until the top is golden brown. Remove from the oven and allow to cool, then cut into bars. Makes about 20 biscuits.

Austria

Austria is leading the way in organic farming, the
first country in the world to establish national regulations. Potatoes
and fruit are among its primary agriculture. And once heavy in meat dishes
like its popular wiener schnitzel, nearly 10% of the population is now vegetarian.

Turkey Schnitzel

This recipe is quick and easy. And you'll get to use a mallet to pound the turkey breast to make it even more tender. Once you master this recipe it will become a family favorite to enjoy with your favorite sauces.

1 pound turkey breast cutlets
½ teaspoon salt
½ teaspoon freshly ground black pepper
½ teaspoon garlic powder
1 cup flour
2 eggs, beaten
2 cups panko breadcrumbs
½ cup grapeseed oil (for frying)
Lemon slices and parsley sprigs (for garnish)

Place the cutlets between 2 pieces of plastic wrap or inside a plastic bag and pound them on both sides with your mallet until they are thin, about ¼ inch thick.

Sprinkle both sides of the cutlets with salt, pepper and garlic powder. Set up a plate with the flour and bowls with the beaten eggs and the breadcrumbs.

First dredge each cutlet in the flour, shaking off any excess. Next dip the cutlet in beaten eggs and finally cover both sides with the breadcrumbs and place the cutlets on a platter.

Using a large skillet, heat the oil. If you drop a tiny bit of breadcrumbs into the oil and it sizzles, the oil is ready to fry the cutlets. Fry the cutlets for about 2 minutes on each side, until they are golden brown. You might have to do this in two batches depending on the size of your skillet. When done place on paper toweling and you are ready to serve. Serves 4.

Apple Strudel

As I see it, strudel can be enjoyed for either breakfast or dessert. And using frozen puff pastry makes an otherwise complicated recipe a breeze.

---

1 package frozen puff pastry (2 sheets) thawed at room temperature according to directions

3 Granny Smith apples, peeled, cored and chopped into half-inch chunks (about 3 to 4 cups)

Juice of 1 lemon

2 tablespoons flour

2 tablespoons raw sugar

2 tablespoons brown sugar

½ cup raisins

½ cup finely chopped walnuts

½ teaspoon cinnamon

1 egg, beaten with 1 teaspoon water for basting

Powdered sugar for dusting

Preheat oven to 350°F. To make the apple filling, place the peeled and chopped apples into a bowl and add the lemon juice, flour, raw sugar, brown sugar, raisins, walnuts and cinnamon and mix well. Set aside for about 15 minutes for the apples to release their juice.

Next line a baking sheet with parchment paper and set aside. Remove the puff pastry from the package. It should be thawed but still cool to the touch. Sprinkle a little flour on a work surface and using a rolling pin, roll out one sheet of the dough evenly until it measures about 10 by 12 inches. Spoon half of the apple mixture into the center of the dough, leaving about 1 inch from all sides.

Lift one side of the pastry and fold over the filling. Then lift the opposite side of the pastry and fold over. Pinch all the sides of the pastry until it is sealed. Using a wide spatula, transfer the strudel to the baking sheet, with the seam side down.

Repeat this procedure on the other pastry sheet.

Brush both strudels with the egg wash and make a few small slits on top for the steam to escape. Place in the preheated oven for 30 to 35 minutes until golden brown. Allow the pastry to cool and dust with powdered sugar. Serve warm with vanilla ice cream or whipped cream, or just as it is. Serves 8 to 10.

Belgium

Belgium is famous for three of my very favorite things: chocolate, waffles and frites, sometimes called French fries, though there is a healthy debate about whether they originated in Belgium or France.

Waffles

Because of the yeast these waffles have a different flavor and texture than the pancake batter you may know. And the great thing about this recipe is that any extras can be frozen and reheated in the toaster for a quick breakfast or snack.

2 cups milk
1 package active dry yeast (¼ ounce)
2 eggs, lightly beaten
½ cup club soda
2½ cups all-purpose flour
1 tablespoon raw sugar
1 teaspoon salt
½ cup butter, melted
Vegetable oil to grease waffle iron

In two separate small saucepans, heat the milk and club soda until just warm.

Remove both pans from the heat. Whisk the yeast into the warm milk and let stand for a few minutes. Then whisk the eggs into the club soda.

In a large bowl, whisk the flour, sugar and salt together. Add the egg mixture and continue whisking. Add the milk mixture and continue whisking until smooth, and finally add the melted butter and blend well. This will be a thin batter. Cover the bowl with a kitchen towel and let the batter stand for at least 1 hour.

Brush your waffle iron lightly with vegetable oil and preheat. My own waffle iron has a red light/green light, which is very helpful for knowing when it is ready to cook. Give the batter another whisk before using a ladle to measure about ½ cup batter per waffle. After making the first waffle you will know the exact right amount to use. Cook according to waffle iron instructions.

Serve waffles with maple syrup or your favorite toppings. Makes about 12 waffles.

Brazil

Nearly 60% of the Amazon rainforest is located in Brazil,
and is filled with all sorts of creatures like toucans, jaguars and even
pink dolphins. The rainforest is also home to some super natural
fruits, like pineapple, guavas, coconuts and avocados.

Feijoada
(Black Bean Stew)

Feijoada is a Portuguese word meaning "beans" and it is the national dish of Brazil. It's traditionally made with all kinds of unusual meats and cooked over a fire in a clay pot. I've made this version according to my own super natural taste buds and it's the perfect meal to enjoy with family and friends on chilly evenings.

2 cups dry black beans, plus water for soaking

8 cups water

1 smoked turkey leg or wing (or regular leg or wing, adding 1 teaspoon of smoked paprika to achieve the smoky flavor)

1 large onion, chopped

3 celery stalks, sliced and diced

1 14-ounce can diced peeled tomatoes

½ cup fresh chopped parsley

3 or 4 bay leaves

½ teaspoon garlic powder

2 teaspoons salt

¼ teaspoon black pepper

(For anyone who likes a really spicy stew, you can add in a chopped chili pepper, like jalapeño or Serrano.)

Soak the beans overnight in a big bowl. Cover them with about 3 inches of water. When you are ready to start cooking the next day, pour the beans into a colander and rinse them well.

Place the beans in a large stockpot; add the 8 cups of water and the smoked turkey wing or leg. Bring to a boil, lower the heat to a simmer, cover and cook for 1 hour. Take off the lid from time to time to stir the beans.

After an hour of cooking, add in the onion, celery, tomatoes, parsley, bay leaves, garlic powder, salt and pepper. Give the pot a good stir, return the lid and cook at the lowest flame for 1 to 1½ hours. I've even cooked it as long as 2 hours. Check the pot from time to time to make sure the beans aren't sticking. The stew should look a little soupy. Remove the smoked turkey before serving with basmati rice and sautéed kale or collard greens (Couve à Mineira). Serves 6 to 8.

Couve à Mineira
(Sautéed Greens)

I call these greens "nutritional dynamite" because they are so good for us. It's the perfect side for the black bean stew.

2 bunches of greens, washed, cut from thick stems and chopped (I like to use Tuscan kale, purple Russian kale or collard greens)

¼ cup olive oil

1 large onion, sliced thin

1 red bell pepper, sliced thin

3 cloves garlic, minced or pressed

1 tablespoon balsamic vinegar

1 teaspoon soy sauce

Salt and black pepper, to taste

After the greens have been washed well and chopped, put them into your steamer basket and steam for 10 minutes, until tender. Set aside for the moment.

Pour oil into a large skillet and sauté the onion until soft. Add the bell pepper and garlic and continue sautéing. Next, stir in the steamed greens. Finally, add the balsamic vinegar, soy sauce, salt and pepper and you are done. Serves 6.

Canada

The second largest country in the world, Canada produces 80% of the world's maple syrup. I don't know about you, but maple syrup is one of my favorite super natural foods. I even love it on my oatmeal.

Poutine with Mushroom Gravy

Poutine is a very popular French-Canadian dish—French fries with gravy and cheese curds. It looks a little funky and the word poutine is actually slang for "a mushy mess." I decided to try to make it healthier. It's a mushy mess that makes everyone ask for seconds.

1½ pounds baby potatoes, quartered

5 tablespoons olive oil

1½ cups vegetable or chicken broth

3 tablespoons flour

1 cup chopped mushrooms (any variety or a mixture)

½ onion, chopped finely

½ cup grated sharp cheddar cheese

2 tablespoons chives, minced (optional)

Salt and pepper to taste

Preheat oven to 375°F. Place the cut potatoes in a bowl and coat them with a tablespoon of the olive oil. Place them on a baking sheet and roast them for 20 to 25 minutes. You can flip them at least once while they are roasting to make sure they get crispy. Crispy is what we are going for here. While the potatoes are roasting you can make the gravy.

In a little mixing bowl or measuring cup mix ½ cup of broth together with the flour until smooth. Set aside.

Put the rest of the olive oil into a skillet and heat it. Stir in the onion and sauté about 3 minutes, until soft. Then add the chopped mushrooms and continue sautéing about 5 minutes more, over medium heat.

Stir in the broth and flour mixture. It will start to thicken right away. Lower the heat and slowly add the remaining cup of broth, stirring constantly to avoid any lumps. Add salt and pepper now.

To serve, put roasted potatoes into a serving dish, top with gravy, then the grated cheese and chives. Serves 4 to 6.

Chile

The world's narrowest country, Chile is also
one of the longest on the planet. They grow a significant
amount of maize and wheat, which when you think about
it are both tall and narrow. Just like Chile.

Cazuela De Ave
(Chicken Stew)

This chicken stew is based on something I once ate in a Chilean restaurant, and it was so tasty all I needed was a good piece of crusty bread to sop up every bit of saucy broth left in the bowl.

8 chicken thighs, with the bone left in and the skin removed

1 tablespoon olive oil

1 tablespoon butter

½ teaspoon paprika

½ teaspoon oregano

¼ teaspoon saffron threads

¼ teaspoon garlic powder

Salt and pepper to taste

1 medium onion, chopped

4 medium carrots, peeled and sliced in rounds

1 cup fresh or frozen peas

½ cup chicken or vegetable broth

Juice of 1 lemon (about 2 tablespoons)

½ cup chopped parsley

Preheat oven to 375°F. You will need a heavy baking dish, like a Dutch oven, with a lid.

This stew requires assembly and here's how you do it. Place the chicken thighs in the bottom of the baking dish. Pour olive oil over the chicken, then dot with butter. Sprinkle with paprika, oregano, saffron, garlic powder, salt and pepper.

Next, throw in the chopped onion, sliced carrots and peas. Pour the broth and lemon juice on top, add the chopped parsley, cover with the lid and put in the oven for 1 hour.

After 1 hour, carefully remove the dish from the oven, remove the lid and give the pot a big stir. Just mix it all up. Put the lid back on and place in the oven for 30 minutes more. Then carefully remove the lid, give the pot another good stir and put back in the oven, uncovered, for another 30 minutes. By this time the meat will fall off the bone and you are going to love the way the vegetables taste. Get out the crusty bread and start soaking up some flavor from Chile. Serves 4 to 6.

Palta Reina
(Queen Avocado)

This is a popular dish in Chile since avocados grow there in abundance. First stuffed with chicken, you can now find this dish made with tuna, salmon or even baby shrimp.

3 large avocados (ripe yet firm)

1½ cups cooked chicken, with skin and bones removed, chopped finely

1 teaspoon fresh chopped herbs, like oregano or thyme

1 tablespoon fresh chopped cilantro

2 tablespoons very finely chopped onion

3 tablespoons mayonnaise

1 tablespoon mustard

Half a lemon

First, cut the avocados neatly in half, lengthwise. Remove the pits, and then carefully remove all the avocado peel. Be careful to leave the avocado in one piece. Squeeze a little lemon juice over each half, and then sprinkle lightly with salt.

In a small mixing bowl, blend together the chicken, herbs, cilantro, onion, mayonnaise and mustard. When the mixture is blended, divide and spoon into each avocado half. Garnish with a sprig of fresh herbs and serve. Serves 6.

China

China is the largest producer of rice in the world. We also have China to thank for dim sum, that popular fried or steamed dumpling that can be savory or sweet. And dim sum literally means "touching the heart" since it was meant to be an appetizer to accompany tea, not a full meal.

Egg Drop Soup

A staple in Chinese restaurants, this soup is a pleasure to make becaue of the "egg threads" and a joy to eat because even with so few ingredients it's quite tasty.

4 cups chicken broth

2 tablespoons tamari soy sauce

1 tablespoon + 1 teaspoon cornstarch

3 eggs, beaten well

8 green onions, sliced very thinly

Pour chicken broth into a saucepan, add the soy sauce, and heat over medium heat. Scoop out about ¼ cup of the broth and mix in the tablespoon of cornstarch until all the lumps are gone, then pour that mixture back into the saucepan and blend well.

Beat the eggs in a small bowl. Next, add the 1 teaspoon of cornstarch and mix in well. Turn off the heat and very, very slowly pour the beaten eggs into the saucepan in a steady stream until the egg forms threads. Add the sliced green onions and serve immediately. Serves 6.

Dan Dan Noodles

A dan dan is used by the street vendors who sell this popular noodle dish. The long bamboo pole has a basket attached to each side and rests on the shoulders. One basket holds the noodles, the other holds the sauce. You don't need a dan dan for this dish, just a big appetite and sense of adventure.

1 package udon noodles (about 12 ounces)

3 tablespoons peanut or olive oil

1 pound ground chicken

1 cup chicken broth

Salt and pepper to taste

1 tablespoon fresh grated ginger root

2 tablespoons rice vinegar

2 tablespoons soy sauce

4 tablespoons sesame paste (tahini)

1 tablespoon raw sugar

Chili oil (optional)

3 or 4 green onions, sliced

½ cup chopped roasted peanuts

Cilantro leaves for garnish

Begin by cooking the noodles according to the directions on the package. When they are done drain them and set them aside.

Pour the peanut oil into a skillet and cook the ground chicken for a few minutes, stirring occasionally. Next, add the chicken stock and all the other ingredients, salt and pepper, the grated ginger root, rice vinegar, soy sauce, tahini sesame paste and raw sugar, making sure you stir after each addition so the sauce is well blended.

Place noodles into each bowl, spoon sauce over the noodles, and garnish each bowl with sliced green onions, chopped peanuts and cilantro. Serves 4 to 6.

Maifun Noodle Salad With Shrimp

This is a perfect summer salad. It's light and refreshing with so much flavor thanks to the variety of sauces, vinegar, ginger and hint of sweetness.

1 pound cooked shrimp, deveined and peeled

2 tablespoons vegetable oil

6 green onions, sliced

¼ red bell pepper, minced

2 cloves garlic

1 cup sliced sugar snap peas

About 5 mushrooms, sliced

½ pound maifun brown rice noodles

1 cup sliced cucumber

DRESSING
Juice of 2 limes (about ⅓ cup)

2 tablespoons fish sauce

1 tablespoon soy sauce

2 tablespoons sweet chili sauce

1 tablespoon toasted sesame oil

1 tablespoon rice vinegar

1 tablespoon sugar

1 tablespoon fresh grated ginger

Begin by cooking the noodles according to the directions on the package. They only take about 2 minutes. When finished cooking, rinse the noodles with cold water, drain well and place in a large salad bowl.

Make the dressing, below. Simply blend all the ingredients together and pour over the shrimp. Set aside for the moment.

Heat the vegetable oil in a skillet and add the onions. Stir for a minute. Next, add the bell pepper and garlic and continue to stir for a minute more. Finally, add the sugar snap peas and the sliced mushrooms and continue stirring for a couple more minutes. Allow to cool for a few minutes.

Put the shrimp that has been marinating in the dressing into the salad bowl, add the cucumber and the vegetable mixture, give it all a big stir and serve. Serves 4 to 6.

Cuba

Cuba is the largest island in the Caribbean and is known for its music, its many colorful classic American cars and its cuisine—a blend of Spanish, African and Native Taino cultures.

Camarones Enchilados
(Shrimp and Rice)

This classic Cuban dish is easy to make and will impress anyone you make it for because it's a little spicy and exotic too.

1 pound fresh shrimp, peeled and deveined (I often use frozen, thawed wild shrimp)

¼ cup olive oil

1 medium onion, chopped

1 green bell pepper, chopped

1 teaspoon oregano

2 cloves of garlic, minced

1 14-ounce can peeled or diced tomatoes

3 or 4 bay leaves

½ cup vegetable broth

1 tablespoon red wine vinegar

2 tablespoons fresh chopped parsley

Salt and pepper

Begin by heating the oil in a skillet. Then sauté the onions until they are soft.

Next, add the bell pepper, garlic and oregano and continue sautéing for a few minutes.

Stir in the canned tomatoes. If you use whole peeled tomatoes you might need to break them up with your spoon. Stir in the bay leaves, then add the vegetable broth and the red wine vinegar. Stir in the fresh chopped parsley. Lower the heat and simmer this sauce for a few minutes more.

Finally, stir in the shrimp and continue to simmer for about 5 minutes, until the shrimp changes color. You don't want to overcook the shrimp here.

Serve with your favorite rice on the side. For this dish I often use jasmine rice. Any long-grain white rice will work well. Serves 4 to 6.

Egypt

Famous for the Great Pyramids and the Sphinx,
Egypt is one of the world's oldest civilizations, and its
capital, Cairo, is one of the largest cities in Africa. The Nile River
provided the water ancient Egyptians needed to thrive and survive.

Koshari

Koshari is the national dish of Egypt. It's served in almost every Egyptian restaurant, every Egyptian home and on the street from vendors. Once you taste it, you will understand why. This recipe is a real family project because there will be something for everyone to do. (And lots of pots to clean up afterwards, but it's worth it.)

---

1 cup long grain rice

2 cups vegetable or chicken broth

1 teaspoon butter

½ teaspoon salt

1 cup brown lentils

2 cups water

2 bay leaves

½ teaspoon garlic powder

1 teaspoon cumin

1 teaspoon paprika

¼ teaspoon black pepper

½ teaspoon salt

2 cups small macaroni noodles (uncooked)

Put 2 cups of vegetable or chicken broth into a small saucepan and bring to a boil. Add the rice, butter and salt, cover with a lid, reduce the heat to simmer and cook for 20 minutes or until all the liquid is absorbed.

Next, rinse the lentils with cold water and place them in another small saucepan. Add the 2 cups of water, the bay leaves, garlic powder, cumin, paprika, salt and black pepper and bring to a boil. Lower the heat to simmer, cover and cook for about 20 minutes, until all the liquid is absorbed and the lentils are tender. (When the lentils are fully cooked, make sure to remove the bay leaves.)

While the lentils are cooking, fill a quart pan with water, add 1 teaspoon of salt and bring to a rolling boil. Stir in the macaroni and cook for about 6 to 8 minutes. Drain and set aside.

Now it's time to prepare the sauce, below. Heat 2 tablespoons of olive oil in a large skillet and sauté the onions and garlic until wilted. Stir in the tomato sauce, then add the cumin, paprika, red wine vinegar, salt and pepper and simmer for about 10 minutes, stirring occasionally. Then set aside for the moment.

To make the crispy onion rings, below, place the sliced onion rings in a bowl. Add the flour and mix until the onions are coated. Heat the grapeseed oil in another skillet and fry the onions until they are dark brown, but not burned. You will have to watch them and keep moving the onions around in the skillet. Use a slotted spoon to remove them from the oil and drain them on a paper towel.

In a large mixing bowl, blend the rice, lentils, macaroni and garbanzo beans. Place the mixture into serving bowls, spoon the tomato sauce on top and add the crispy onions for garnish. Hooray! You are finally ready to enjoy this amazing dish. Serves 8.

FOR THE TOMATO SAUCE

2 tablespoons olive oil

1 medium onion, chopped

3 cloves garlic, minced

1 28-ounce can tomato sauce

1 teaspoon cumin

1 teaspoon paprika

2 tablespoons red wine vinegar

1 teaspoon salt

½ teaspoon black pepper

1 15-ounce can garbanzo beans, drained

FOR CRISPY ONION GARNISH

2 large onions, thinly sliced in rings

2 tablespoons flour

¼ cup grapeseed oil for frying

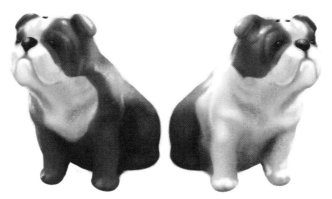

England

England is a country that I love so much—for its beautiful and lush gardens, its architecture, its museums, castles, rivers and for a good cup of tea. Long considered to be more on the bland side of things, English cuisine has come a very long way since I first visited. I'm including some of my favorite more traditional recipes for you to enjoy.

Popovers

Once my mother learned to make popovers she made them all the time. She even had two special popover pans, although you can easily use nonstick muffin tins. As they bake, the popovers rise up quite tall and usually flop to one side.

Popovers are light as air and hollow inside, and they can be eaten for breakfast with butter and jam or they can be served with dinner.

3 eggs, beaten well
1 cup milk
3 tablespoons vegetable oil
1 cup unbleached flour, sifted
½ teaspoon salt

Preheat oven to 400°F. Lightly grease your popover pan or muffin tin with oil. In a medium bowl beat the eggs, milk and oil until well blended. Sift 1 cup of flour into the egg, milk and oil mixture and beat until smooth. This is one time when you do not want to over-beat the mixture.

Pour the batter into the popover pan or muffin tins until they are just half-full. Bake for 25 to 30 minutes until they are golden brown and serve them hot. Makes 6 popovers.

Vegetarian Nut Loaf

Many years ago I went to a vegetarian restaurant in London called Crank's. I tasted their nut loaf and it was better than any meat loaf I'd ever had. I just had to recreate it. And this recipe is the result.

1½ cups cooked brown rice

1½ cups walnuts, chopped finely

½ cup cashew nuts, chopped finely

2 tablespoons butter

1 tablespoon olive oil

1 medium onion, chopped

1 clove garlic, minced

6 ounces mushrooms, chopped

½ teaspoon dried thyme

½ teaspoon rubbed sage

¼ cup chopped parsley

2 tablespoons tamari soy sauce

2 eggs, beaten

1 cup cottage cheese

1½ cups grated cheese
   (any firm cheese)

½ teaspoon salt

¼ teaspoon black pepper

Parchment paper

Preheat oven to 375°F. Melt butter in a skillet and then add the olive oil. Sauté the onion until soft, then add the garlic and mushrooms and continue sautéing until everything is well cooked, about 6 minutes total. Stir in the tamari, herbs, salt and pepper.

Put the rice into a large mixing bowl. Add the chopped nuts, the onion/mushroom mixture, the beaten eggs and the cheeses. Blend this mixture well.

Grease a loaf pan with butter. Line the pan with parchment paper and grease the paper with butter.

Carefully put the loaf mixture into the loaf pan and pat it down evenly.

Bake in the oven for about 1 hour and 15 minutes. Remove from the oven and allow the loaf to cool for about 15 minutes. Use the edges of the parchment paper to lift the loaf out of the pan and turn it upside down on a platter. Remove the paper and it is ready to serve. Serves 6.

Cream of Cauliflower Soup

This soup is creamy white and so pretty, it looks like puffy clouds. And no, you're not dreaming when you see whipping cream as one of the ingredients.

1 large head of cauliflower

2 tablespoons butter

1 tablespoon olive oil

1 medium onion, chopped

2 tablespoons unbleached flour

3 cups vegetable or chicken broth

1 cup whipping cream or half and half

Salt and white pepper, to taste

¼ cup grated Parmesan cheese

Chives for garnish

Begin by washing the cauliflower and trimming off the outer leaves. Ask an adult to help you cut out the center core, then it will be easy to break the cauliflower into large florets. Set them aside for the moment.

In a medium-sized stockpot, melt the butter and then add the olive oil.

Stir in the chopped onion and sauté a few minutes until soft. Next, stir in the flour and then add the broth slowly. Blend well to break up any lumps. When the broth starts to boil add the cauliflower florets and lower the heat. Cover the pot and simmer for 15 minutes or until the cauliflower is very tender.

Now remove from the stove and stir in the cream and salt and pepper.

Sometimes broth already has salt, so taste to make sure you don't overdo it.

Now use a cup to put the soup into the blender. You will have to do this in about three batches. Blend until creamy. Return the soup to a pot and stir in the Parmesan. Sprinkle each serving with chopped chives. Serves 6.

Lemon Curd

If you enjoy a good lemon meringue pie (as I do), then you will love lemon curd. It's sweet and tart and creamy too. And it's a great lemony gift. Place it in a pretty jar, tie it with a little ribbon and you'll make someone very happy.

_____

3 eggs, beaten
⅔ cup raw sugar
¾ cup fresh lemon juice
1 tablespoon lemon zest
½ cup unsalted butter, cut into small pieces

In a small saucepan, whisk together the beaten eggs, sugar, lemon juice and zest. When well blended, heat over medium heat and slowly add the butter. Keep stirring until mixture thickens and just starts to bubble, about 6 minutes. Pour into a bowl, cover and refrigerate for 1 hour. Then it's ready to use on scones, popovers or anything else you can think of. Sometimes I just eat it with a spoon, but don't tell anyone.

Licky Sticky Pudding

I first tried this tasty dessert when visiting friends in Bath, England and never forgot it.

12 dates, chopped in little pieces
1 cup water
1 cup dark brown sugar, lightly packed
½ cup butter, at room temperature
3 eggs, lightly beaten
1 teaspoon vanilla extract
1½ cups white whole-wheat flour
1 teaspoon baking powder
1 teaspoon baking soda

Preheat oven to 350°F. Place the chopped dates into a small saucepan and pour the water over them. Bring mixture to a boil, give it a stir, then remove it from the heat and allow it to cool.

In the bowl of your mixer, cream the butter until smooth, then add the brown sugar and continue until the mixture is creamy. Add the beaten eggs and continue mixing. It will be necessary to turn off the mixer and scrape down the sides of the bowl at least once before adding the vanilla.

Next, add the flour, a bit at a time, and then add the baking powder and baking soda. Finally, stir in the date and water mixture and blend until smooth. The batter will be thin.

Pour batter into a greased loaf pan and bake in the oven for 50 to 60 minutes. It is done when you insert a knife into the cake and it comes out clean.

TOFFEE SAUCE
½ cup butter
1 teaspoon vanilla extract
1 cup whipping cream
1 cup dark brown sugar, lightly packed

Melt the butter in a small saucepan. Then stir in the vanilla, cream and brown sugar. Bring mixture to a boil, lower the heat to a simmer and cook for about 10 to 15 minutes, stirring constantly, until it starts to get sticky, thick and shiny. This is one time when you have to stay near the stove and continue stirring, otherwise it could boil over and make a right old mess.

To serve, slice the loaf cake and pour a good spoonful of sauce over each slice. Serves 6 to 8.

English Trifle

Trifle is a traditional English dessert that is a national favorite. There are many ways to make it. Feel free to experiment with different kinds of cake, jam and fruit. This dessert is assembled in layers. Using a glass bowl allows you to see all the layers.

CUSTARD

3 tablespoons raw sugar

1½ tablespoons cornstarch

2 eggs

1 teaspoon vanilla extract

2½ cups milk

WHIPPED CREAM

1½ cups whipping cream

3 tablespoons powdered sugar

1 teaspoon vanilla extract

1 pound of carrot cake or pound cake

¾ cup natural raspberry jam

2 cups sliced strawberries

2 bananas, sliced

½ cup toasted slivered almonds

Whisk the sugar, cornstarch and eggs in a saucepan. Slowly stir in the milk and cook, stirring constantly, over medium heat, until the mixture begins to thicken, about 10 to 15 minutes. Stir in the vanilla extract and set aside to cool.

Next, in a mixing bowl, whip the cream until soft peaks form. Beat in the powdered sugar and the vanilla and continue whipping until stiff. Place in the refrigerator until you are ready to assemble the trifle.

Next, cut the cake into slices ¼ inch thick and place half of the slices on the bottom of a large glass bowl, about a 2½-quart size. Spread half of the raspberry jam on top. Next, pour half of the custard over the cake, then half of the sliced fruit. Repeat this process: cake, jam, custard, fruit. Save a few whole strawberries to decorate the top.

Finally, spoon the whipped cream over the top, sprinkle with the toasted almonds and decorate with the berries. Chill until ready to serve. Serves 6 to 8.

France

Paris is one of my favorite cities.
It's so beautiful and there is so much to see.
I love walking there. And even though the French eat
about 7 million snails each year, I do love the food there.
They have some of the best bread and cheese anywhere in the world.

Cherry Clafoutis

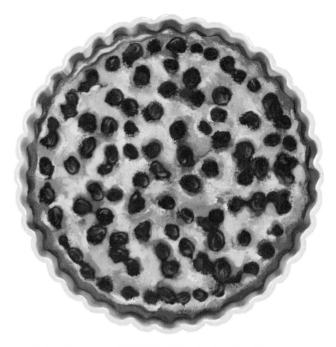

Clafoutis is classically made with cherries but I have often used berries or plums. Make sure the cherries are pitted. We don't want anyone to break a tooth on a cherry pit.

---

2 tablespoons butter

2 cups pitted fresh sweet cherries

½ cup all-purpose flour

½ cup raw sugar

¼ teaspoon cinnamon

¼ teaspoon salt

4 eggs

1 cup milk

1 teaspoon vanilla extract

Preheat oven to 400°F. Melt the butter in a 9-inch cast iron or stainless steel skillet. Make sure the butter is spread over the bottom of the skillet. Then add the cherries evenly over the bottom.

Next mix the dry ingredients (flour, sugar, cinnamon and salt) in a mixing bowl. In another bowl, or even the electric blender, beat together the eggs, milk and vanilla extract. Slowly blend the egg and milk mixture into the dry mixture, a bit at a time. Mix or whisk until you have a smooth batter. Pour this batter over the cherries in the skillet and place in the oven.

Bake for about 20 to 25 minutes. When the clafoutis is done the edges will look puffed up and golden brown. You can serve this warm from the oven with a dusting of powdered sugar, or with whipped cream. Serves 4 to 6.

Salade Niçoise

This is a popular main course salad in France and is enjoyed all over the world. It is especially great in the summer when green beans, tomatoes and basil are all fresh from the garden.

1 pound fresh ahi tuna or good quality canned solid albacore tuna, drained

1 pound green beans, trimmed and cut

1 pound new potatoes, cut in bite-sized pieces

¼ cup fresh basil, chopped

1 cup cherry tomatoes, cut in half

½ cup pitted Kalamata olives

Salt

Freshly ground black pepper

3 tablespoons balsamic vinegar

3 tablespoons olive oil

Lettuce leaves, for serving

For this salad, we are going to prepare all the ingredients and then put them all together. Start with the tuna first. Drizzle a little bit of olive oil on the tuna and then salt and pepper. Place under the broiler and broil each side a few minutes, so that it is just barely pink inside. Put aside to cool.

Next, trim and cut the green beans into about 2-inch pieces. Steam the green beans until they are just tender, about 10 minutes. Then remove them from the heat. Don't let them overcook, since the beautiful green color will change. You can even pour cold water over them to stop them from cooking. Set these aside to cool.

Next, steam the potatoes until tender, about 8 minutes. Set aside to cool.

In a large salad bowl mix together the green beans, potatoes, basil, cherry tomatoes and olives. Break the tuna into pieces and add to bowl. Sprinkle with salt and a grind of black pepper, then the balsamic vinegar and olive oil. Give it all a good toss and serve on lettuce leaves. Serves 4 to 6.

Endive and Boursin Appetizer

This is the perfect, easy-to-make, delicious appetizer. Boursin cheese is creamy, sometimes flavored with garlic or fine herbs, and comes in a dome shape. It's great on crackers but the French really like it on endive, especially the Belgian endive variety. Endive is a leaf vegetable that belongs to the daisy family and when the leaves are removed they resemble canoes, perfect for filling with all kinds of yummy things.

---

2 or 3 Belgian endive
1 package Boursin cheese
Dried cranberries

Begin by washing the endive and patting it dry. Carefully remove the leaves, one at a time, and lay on a platter. Place 1 teaspoon of Boursin cheese into each endive leaf and garnish with a dried cranberry. Serves 6.

Potage Parmentier

This is my favorite soup to make in the winter because it just warms me up from the inside. You can use a vegetable broth if you prefer to make an extra healthy version.

2 tablespoons butter

4 leeks, cleaned and mostly white part, sliced

2 shallots, minced (about ½ cup)

3 large russet potatoes, peeled and chopped into small pieces (about 4 cups)

2 tablespoons flour

4 cups chicken broth, unsalted

1 teaspoon sea salt

¼ teaspoon white pepper

Sour cream or plain Greek yogurt, optional

Since leeks are root vegetables they tend to be dirty so it's important to wash them well. Cut through half of the dark green part and discard in your compost. Next, cut the roots part off the bottom and discard, much like a green onion. You will only be using the white and pale green parts of the leek. Now, carefully slice lengthwise, so it splits in half. Run the split leek under the water, making sure all of the dirt goes down the sink. Place the leeks on a paper towel to drain before slicing.

Melt the butter in a heavy-bottomed saucepan. Stir in the leeks and sauté a few minutes. Stir in the shallots and sauté a few minutes more, stirring until the leeks and shallots are wilted. Next, stir in the flour and add the chicken broth slowly and blend well. This is where you stir and stir and you will see the broth start to thicken.

Add the potatoes, salt and pepper, cover and cook over medium heat for 20 to 30 minutes, stirring occasionally so nothing sticks on the bottom.

Top each bowl of soup with a dollop (a blob) of sour cream or plain Greek yogurt before serving. Serves 4 to 6.

Germany

Even though there are over three hundred types of bread
in Germany, most people associate the country with pretzels.
Germans eat pretzels for breakfast, snacks and dinner, and children
have even been known to wear them around their neck
like a necklace on New Year's Day for good luck.

Bavarian Potato Salad

Almost every country I know of has its own version of potato salad. Germany is pretty famous for its mustardy variety. It's a perfect dish to take to a potluck or on a picnic.

2 pounds new or Yukon Gold potatoes, scrubbed and cut into bite-sized pieces

2 tablespoons olive oil

1 onion, chopped

4 ounces turkey bacon, diced

3 tablespoons whole-grain mustard

3 tablespoons red wine vinegar

2 teaspoons sugar

3 tablespoons finely chopped chives or parsley

Salt and freshly ground black pepper

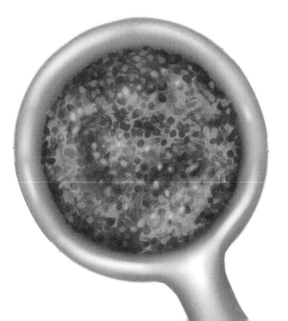

First, steam the potatoes until tender, about 15 to 20 minutes. Make sure to steam because if they are boiled they will get mushy. When the potatoes are cooked, drain them in a colander and place in salad bowl.

Next, add the olive oil to a skillet and heat it. Then sauté the onion. When the onions are soft, add the diced bacon pieces and continue sautéing until onions and bacon get a little crispy. Set aside for the moment.

In a small bowl, whisk together the mustard, vinegar and sugar. Add the onion and bacon to the potatoes, and then add the mustard sauce. Add the chives or parsley, salt and pepper (only fresh-grind will do) and mix everything together carefully using a wooden spoon so the potatoes don't break up. Serves 6.

Apple Pancake

This is a really big pancake that is baked in the oven. It's great for breakfast, brunch, or even dessert. I love to use my favorite old cast-iron skillet but any ovenproof skillet will work, and your blender is perfect for making the batter.

5 eggs

1½ cups milk

1 cup white whole-wheat flour

3 tablespoons raw sugar

½ teaspoon salt

3 Granny Smith apples, peeled, cored and sliced

½ teaspoon fresh grated nutmeg

3 tablespoons brown sugar

Preheat oven to 425°F. Place eggs and milk in the jar of your blender or in a bowl and beat. Add the flour, 2 teaspoons of the sugar, salt and nutmeg and blend until smooth. Set aside.

Next, melt butter in the skillet and use a pastry brush to make sure the sides of the skillet are coated in butter. Stir in the apples and sprinkle with the remaining tablespoon of sugar. Sauté the apples in the butter until they soften, for about 5 minutes. Carefully remove the skillet from the heat. (Get your mitts on.)

Now carefully pour the batter evenly over the apples. Sprinkle the brown sugar on top and place in the oven. Bake for 30 to 35 minutes until the pancake is golden brown and puffed-up.

Serve warm from the oven with maple syrup. Serves 4 to 6.

Creamed Spinach

This vegetable dish is so popular in Germany, families eat it at least once a week. It's one of my favorite ways to eat spinach. If you weren't a spinach lover before, you soon will be.

1¼ pounds fresh spinach (about 2 bunches)

2 tablespoons butter

½ medium onion, chopped

1 or 2 cloves garlic, minced

½ cup heavy whipping cream

¼ teaspoon grated nutmeg

½ teaspoon salt

¼ teaspoon black pepper

Wash the spinach well and cut off all the stems. Then steam the spinach for just a few minutes, until the leaves are wilted. Put the spinach into a colander or large strainer and let it drain. Use the back of a wooden spoon to press as much water out of the spinach as you can. Then, when it is cool, chop it well and set it aside.

Melt butter in a medium-sized saucepan. Stir in the onion and garlic and sauté until soft, about 3 or 4 minutes. Next, stir in the chopped spinach, cream, salt, pepper and nutmeg and stir over medium heat for about 5 minutes more until the cream is mostly absorbed. Serves 4 to 6.

Greece

The Greek diet is the closest you can get to a
super natural way of eating, consisting primarily of
vegetables, olive oil, nuts, fish, grains and
small amounts of meat. Opa!

Pastitsio
(Baked Pasta)

This is a famous Greek dish I made healthier by using ground turkey. There's always something special about the gooeyness of pasta baked in the oven, and this one is packed with flavor.

1 pound whole-wheat penne pasta

3 tablespoons olive oil

2 medium onions, chopped

1¼ pounds ground turkey

½ teaspoon garlic powder

½ teaspoon salt

2 tablespoons tamari soy sauce

2 tablespoons Worcestershire sauce

½ teaspoon nutmeg

CHEESE SAUCE

2 tablespoons butter

1 tablespoon olive oil

2 tablespoons flour

3 cups milk

½ teaspoon nutmeg

½ teaspoon salt

⅛ teaspoon white pepper

2 cups grated mild cheddar

Preheat oven to 375°F. Begin by cooking the penne pasta according to package directions, drain and put in a greased casserole or baking dish, approximately 9 x 14-inch size. Set aside.

Next, put the olive oil into a large skillet and sauté the onions until very soft. Stir in the ground turkey and break up with a spoon. When turkey is thoroughly cooked, add the garlic powder, salt, tamari soy sauce, Worcestershire sauce and nutmeg. Put this turkey mixture on top of the pasta. To make the cheese sauce, melt the butter in a saucepan and stir in the olive oil. Then add the flour and stir for 1 minute, blending it well. Slowly add the milk and use a whisk to blend it well so there aren't any lumps. Cook this sauce over a medium flame for about 5 minutes, until the sauce thickens. Then add nutmeg, salt, pepper and cheese. Blend in well and carefully pour the cheese sauce over the turkey and pasta.

Bake in the oven for 20 minutes or until it starts to bubble. Serves 6 to 8.

Tahini Dressing

This is an easy dressing to make for any salad or even as a sauce for steamed vegetables. It tastes good in wraps too. It's tangy and velvety and delicious.

¼ cup tahini (sesame paste)
1 clove garlic
1 tablespoon lemon juice
1 tablespoon tamari soy sauce
¼ teaspoon ground cumin
2 to 3 tablespoons water

Put all ingredients into a small bowl or mini food processor and blend well.

You can store any unused dressing in your refrigerator for up to one week.

Makes approximately ⅓ cup dressing.

SUPER NATURAL FAMILY COOKBOOK

Holland

Holland is known as the flower shop
of the world because they export so many bulbs,
especially tulips. Seeing wooden shoes and windmills
always brings Holland to my mind. There are more bicycles
per person here than in any other country in the world—more bikes
than people, which is great for healthy bodies and a healthy planet too.

Stamppot
(Dutch Kale Hash with Sausage)

Stamppot is not exactly a stew but it is a winter dish that Dutch people like so much they eat it all year long.

2 pounds russet potatoes, peeled and quartered

1 bunch kale, stems removed and chopped

4 tablespoons butter

1 cup milk

1 teaspoon salt

¼ teaspoon white pepper

2 tablespoons olive oil

1 onion, chopped

¾ pound smoked chicken or turkey sausage, sliced into rounds

1 tablespoon balsamic vinegar

Freshly ground black pepper

Steam the kale for about ten minutes, remove from the heat and set aside.

Next, boil the potatoes. Place the potatoes into a pot and cover them with water. Add ½ teaspoon salt and bring to a boil, uncovered. Boil the potatoes until they are fork-tender, about 15 minutes. Carefully drain the potatoes into a colander and then return them to the pot. Add 3 tablespoons of the butter, milk and salt and pepper, and mash potatoes until smooth and creamy. Set aside.

Add olive oil and 1 tablespoon butter to a heavy skillet. When the butter has melted, stir in the onions and sauté them until they start to get a little brown and crispy. (Not burned.) Then stir in the sliced sausage and continue stirring until the sausages are heated through and start to brown. Finally, stir in the steamed kale and mix all together well. Stir in the balsamic vinegar and pepper and you are ready to assemble this dish.

Put a good scoop of mashed potatoes in the middle of a plate or large bowl and smash them down in the middle. Then put a generous spoon of the kale/sausage mixture right in the middle. Serves 4 to 6.

Gingerbread

You've probably nibbled a gingerbread cookie, but have you ever tried a gingerbread cake? If you serve a chunk of this spicy cake with sweet whipped cream or vanilla ice cream, it's a grown-up dessert that pleases everyone.

3 eggs

½ cup vegetable oil

1 cup packed brown sugar

½ cup molasses

1 teaspoon vanilla extract

1 tablespoon fresh grated ginger root

1½ cups white whole-wheat flour

½ teaspoon salt

2 tablespoons ground ginger

1 tablespoon cinnamon

½ teaspoon nutmeg

½ teaspoon baking soda

½ teaspoon baking powder

Preheat oven to 350°F. Begin by greasing a 9-inch square baking pan. Then crack the 3 eggs into the bowl of your mixer and beat well. Add the vegetable oil, brown sugar, molasses, vanilla extract and the fresh grated ginger. (Molasses is sticky so it helps to measure it after measuring out the oil. It will just slide out of your measuring cup.) Blend until the mixture is smooth and creamy. Set aside.

In a separate bowl, blend the dry ingredients—the flour, salt, spices, baking soda and baking powder. Slowly add the dry ingredients to the egg mixture. Blend until smooth. Don't forget to scrape down the sides of the bowl as you are mixing.

Pour batter into the prepared baking dish and bake for 30 minutes, or until a knife inserted in the cake comes out clean. Serves 8.

Hungary

Bordered by seven neighboring countries,
Hungary is most famous for a spice called paprika.
Paprika is a bright red pepper that is dried and ground
into spice. It contains a good amount of
vitamin C to help us stay healthy.

Chicken Paprikash

Get ready to cry. Because this recipe has three onions in it. By the time it's finished and you've eaten it, you won't be crying anymore. You will be licking the plate.

3 pounds chicken pieces like thighs and legs, with bone in and skin on

3 large onions, sliced thin

3 tablespoons butter

1 tablespoon olive oil

3 tablespoons sweet paprika (called Hungarian paprika or paprika dulce)

2 cups chicken broth

1 teaspoon salt

½ teaspoon black pepper

1½ cups sour cream or plain Greek yogurt

1 tablespoon flour

1 12-ounce package of wide egg noodles or wide whole-grain noodles

Melt butter in a large Dutch oven or heavy stockpot. Add olive oil, then heat until sizzling. Salt and pepper the chicken pieces, then add them to the butter/oil mixture and brown the chicken, about 3 or 4 minutes on each side. Using a slotted spoon, remove chicken pieces to a plate and set aside.

Next, add onions to the pot and sauté them until soft, about 5 minutes. Be sure to scrape the brown bits from the bottom of the pot because there is a lot of flavor in those bits. Stir in the paprika, chicken broth, salt and pepper and return the chicken, placing pieces on top of the onions. Cover with a lid, lower the heat to simmer and cook for 1 hour. Halfway through the cooking, turn the chicken pieces over.

Just before the paprikash is done, boil and drain the noodles according to the directions on the package.

Remove the chicken pieces again, this time to a clean plate. Stir 1 tablespoon of flour into the yogurt and mix well. Slowly stir the flour/yogurt mixture into the onion/broth mixture until well blended and smooth. If it looks at all lumpy, use your whisk to blend. Simmer this sauce, stirring well, for about 5 to 6 minutes. Stir in the noodles and serve with a piece of chicken on each serving. Serves 6.

India

Though I have been to India twice and spent months there,
it is still so vast and has such a huge population there is always more
to see and experience. Indian food could be one of my favorite cuisines.
Cows are sacred in India so a lot of the people are vegetarians. And the
practice of yoga, popular around the world, originated in India.

Cauliflower and Garbanzo Bean Curry

This dish is ideal for the vegetarians in the family. Hopefully most of the ingredients are already in your pantry for a spontaneous meat-free day.

1 tablespoon olive oil

1 tablespoon butter

1 onion, chopped

2 cloves garlic, minced

½ teaspoon brown mustard seeds

2 teaspoons mild curry powder

1 15-ounce can of diced tomatoes

½ cup water

1 medium cauliflower, cut into bite-sized florets

2 cups cooked garbanzo beans

1 teaspoon salt

¼ teaspoon black pepper

Add olive oil and butter to a skillet and heat until sizzling. Add chopped onion and garlic and sauté until soft, about 4 to 5 minutes. Next, stir in the mustard seeds and curry powder. Then add the canned tomato and cook for a few minutes more.

Add the water and cauliflower florets, stir well and cover the skillet with a lid. Lower the heat and cook for 10 minutes. Next, add the garbanzo beans, give the pot a good stir, cover and cook for 10 minutes more. Add salt and pepper and serve with brown rice for a delicious, simple meal. Serves 4 to 6.

Mulligatawny Soup

The name of this soup is so much fun to say that Dr. Seuss wrote about a "scraggle-foot mulligatawny." I first tasted this soup when I was traveling in India, and it was especially memorable since I was at a beautiful palace in the middle of a lake. And that's why I wanted to recreate it for you.

2 tablespoons butter

1 medium onion, chopped

2 tablespoons garam masala (an Indian spice)

4 cups chicken broth

1 teaspoon salt

¼ teaspoon black pepper

3 celery stalks, chopped

2 carrots, peeled and diced small

1 boneless, skinless chicken breast, cut into small pieces (try using your kitchen scissors here)

½ cup basmati rice

1 cup plain Greek yogurt

Parsley, for garnish

Melt the butter in a stockpot and then sauté the onion over medium heat until soft. Stir in the garam masala and blend well, making sure it doesn't stick to the bottom. Slowly add the chicken broth, salt and pepper, celery, carrots, chicken and rice, lower the heat, cover and cook for 20 minutes. Remove from the heat and let the soup stand for about 10 minutes. Slowly stir in the yogurt, blend well and serve with a little chopped parsley in each bowl. Serves 4 to 6.

Coconut Fish Curry

Curry powder, a mixture of many different spices, was first exported to England in the 18th century, a long time ago. England was where I first fell in love with food from India at the many Indian restaurants in London. Curries remain one of my favorite dishes to this day. There is actually a curry tree, and its leaves are used in cooking.

1½ pounds tilapia fillets, cut into bite-sized pieces

3 tablespoons olive oil

½ teaspoon mustard seeds

1 onion, chopped

2 cloves of garlic, minced

1 14-ounce can coconut milk

Juice of 2 limes

1 tablespoon fresh grated ginger

1 tablespoon mild curry powder

1 teaspoon salt

¼ teaspoon pepper

Cilantro for garnish

Pour the olive oil into a skillet and heat it. Add the mustard seeds and fry them for a minute until they pop a little. Then add the onion and stir over medium heat until it is soft. Next, add the garlic and cook a minute or two longer.

Pour the coconut milk into the pan, then the lime juice, ginger and curry powder and stir well. Continue cooking over medium heat for a few minutes more. Next, add the pieces of fish and cook for 5 minutes more.

Finally, add the salt and pepper and serve with basmati rice. Garnish with sprigs of cilantro. Serves 4 to 6.

Perfect Basmati Rice

Basmati rice comes as white rice and as brown rice. Though I advocate for eating whole grains, sometimes I just really love white rice, especially if it's jasmine or basmati. So once in a while something I make just goes better and more traditionally with white rice. Here we go:

2 cups water
1 tablespoon butter
½ teaspoon salt
1 cup basmati rice

Pour water into a saucepan that has a lid and add the butter and salt. When the water comes to a full boil, stir in the rice, lower the heat to simmer, cover with the lid and set your timer for 20 minutes. You do not need to open the lid to check on it until the timer goes off. Then turn off the heat, fluff the rice with a wooden spoon and let it stand for a few minutes before serving. It will be perfect. Serves 4.

Mango Lassi
(Indian Yogurt Drink)

The first time I had mango lassi was in India. I never forgot it. As an Armenian, I grew up with a yogurt drink called tan, but we never made ours with fruit. You can experiment with different kinds of fruit and different varieties of yogurt.

½ cup plain yogurt

1½ cups cold water

Flesh of 1 ripe mango (approximately 1 cup, chopped)

Combine all ingredients in the jar of an electric blender and blend until smooth. Serves 2.

Ireland

Ireland's nickname is The Emerald Isle because it's an
island and it's so green. It's so green because it rains a lot.
It's still one of my favorite places because I just love
the people and there aren't any snakes.

Poundies
(Mashed Potatoes)

When I think of Irish food I think of potatoes. This version of Irish potatoes, also called champ, makes the best mashed potatoes ever and is super easy. Poundies are the perfect thing to serve on St. Patrick's Day or even Thanksgiving.

2 pounds russet potatoes, peeled and cut into chunks

⅔ cup milk

3 tablespoons butter

8 green onions, sliced very thin, including part of the green

½ teaspoon salt

¼ teaspoon white pepper

Extra butter

In a stockpot, cover the cut potatoes with cold water, add 1 teaspoon salt and bring to a boil. Cook until potatoes are fork-tender. Drain the potatoes and return them to the pot.

Next, put milk, butter and sliced green onions into a small saucepan and heat over a medium flame until the mixture bubbles. Pour this mixture into the pot and mash the potatoes until they are smooth and creamy. Add salt and pepper.

When serving, make a volcano shape out of the potatoes with a well in the middle and add an extra spoon of butter into the well. Serves 6.

Wheaten Bread

This is a traditional family recipe from my Irish friend Hazel.

4 cups whole-wheat flour
1½ cups plain flour
⅔ cup rolled oats
2 teaspoons raw sugar
2 teaspoons baking soda
Pinch salt
2 cups buttermilk

Preheat oven to 400°F. In a large bowl, mix together the flours, oats, sugar, baking soda and salt and make a well in the center.

Gradually add just enough of the buttermilk to mix into a soft but not sticky dough and knead lightly until just smooth.

Shape into a round, place on greased baking tray and cut a deep cross in the top.

Bake for about 60 minutes until risen and golden and the bread sounds hollow when tapped on the base.

Serve in slices with butter and a good spoonful of homemade jam. Serves 6.

Israel

Israel is one of the healthiest countries in the world, thanks to the protein-packed falafel (Israel's "national dish") and flavor-punched breakfast salads. Also, dates are plentiful there and are considered a superfruit.

Israeli Couscous Salad

Israeli couscous is different from Moroccan couscous. It looks like little pearls. You can follow this recipe exactly for a lively side dish, or you can add all kinds of things like cherry tomatoes, feta cheese, pine nuts or raisins.

1 tablespoon olive oil

1½ cups Israeli couscous

1¾ cups water or broth (vegetable or chicken)

⅓ cup purple onion, chopped finely

½ red bell pepper, chopped

1 cup sliced cucumber (I love the Persian varieties)

2 tablespoons chopped parsley

2 tablespoons fresh mint leaves, finely chopped

Zest of 1 lemon

> **DRESSING**
> **Juice of 1 large lemon**
> **¼ cup olive oil**
> **1 teaspoon honey**
> **¼ teaspoon garlic powder**
> **Salt and pepper to taste**

Begin by cooking the couscous. This can be done in advance so the grains have time to cool. Add the tablespoon of olive oil to a 2-quart saucepan and stir in the couscous. Heat to medium and stir until the couscous is slightly browned. Slowly add the water or broth and bring to a boil. Reduce the heat to a simmer, cover with a lid and cook for about 12 minutes, until the liquid is absorbed. Set aside and prepare the dressing by combining all of the ingredients.

When the couscous has cooled, place in a salad bowl and add the chopped onion, bell pepper, cucumber, parsley, mint leaves and lemon zest. Next, add the dressing, toss well and serve. Serves 4 to 6.

Shakshuka
(Middle Eastern Poached Eggs)

If you're looking for something different for breakfast, this is it. Shakshuka means "a mixture" and this version of huevos rancheros has become the most popular breakfast dish in Israel, where it is typically served in a sizzling skillet.

3 tablespoons olive oil

1 medium onion, chopped

2 cloves garlic, minced

1 green bell pepper, chopped

4 large ripe tomatoes, chopped

1 teaspoon tamari soy sauce

1 teaspoon ground cumin

1 teaspoon salt

½ teaspoon black pepper

4 eggs

Pour olive oil into a skillet and heat. Stir in the chopped onion and sauté until very soft, then add the minced garlic and the chopped bell pepper and continue sautéing over medium heat for about 5 minutes. The onion/pepper mixture should be quite well cooked.

Next, add the chopped tomatoes, tamari, cumin, salt and pepper and continue to cook over medium heat for another 5 minutes.

Now crack the eggs, one at a time, into a small cup and carefully slip each egg on top of the tomato sauce. Spread the eggs out evenly. Put a cover on the skillet and cook for 5 minutes more. They will start to look like "over easy" eggs.

Serve with whole-wheat pita bread to soak up the sauce. Serves 4.

Italy

Pasta is firmly rooted in Italian culture, with
nearly 300 different names for pasta shapes. While I'm
not including any pasta recipes in this section, you'll see
several recipes with tomatoes, another essential element in
Italian cooking. There's even a tomato museum
in Parma dedicated to the savory fruit.

Minestrone

Minestrone is a classic Italian vegetable soup, usually made with whatever vegetables are in season. Those extra servings of veggies will help keep the whole family healthy.

6 cups vegetable or chicken broth

1 medium onion, chopped

3 medium carrots, diced

¼ pound green beans, cut into 1-inch pieces (approximately 2 cups)

¼ pound baby potatoes, diced (Yukon Gold or red)

1 tablespoon dried basil

1 teaspoon dried oregano

½ teaspoon garlic powder

1 15-ounce can diced tomatoes

1 teaspoon salt

¼ teaspoon black pepper

1 15-ounce can cannellini, drained (white kidney beans)

1 cup whole-wheat fusilli or rotelli pasta

2 small or 1 medium zucchini, sliced in rounds

Grated Parmesan cheese, at least 1 cup

In a large stockpot, bring broth to a boil. Add the onion, carrots, green beans, potatoes, canned tomatoes, garlic powder, basil, oregano, salt and pepper. Lower heat to medium, cover with a lid and cook for 10 minutes.

Next, add the pasta and the beans and cook an additional 10 minutes. Turn off the heat, add the zucchini, cover and let stand for 10 minutes. Serve with grated Parmesan in each bowl.

Tip: This is a soup you can experiment with by using different kinds of pasta, vegetables and beans. Serves 6.

Bruschetta

Bruschetta is one of Italy's favorite snack foods. Basically it's grilled bread rubbed with garlic and olive oil. In the summer, when tomatoes and basil are at their best, they make a wonderful addition to this appetizer.

---

1 long loaf of crusty Italian or French bread, sliced and toasted

2 cups chopped ripe tomatoes

2 cloves fresh garlic, minced

½ cup fresh basil leaves, chopped

1 tablespoon balsamic vinegar

1 tablespoon extra virgin olive oil

In a bowl, mix the tomatoes, garlic, basil, vinegar and olive oil, and pile on toasted or grilled slices of bread. Serves 6.

Insalata Caprese
(Appetizer)

Caprese means "in the style of Capri," a beautiful little island off the coast of Italy. It is usually served on a plate but this salad on a stick is fun as well as tasty.

Bamboo skewers
Fresh mozzarella balls (ciliegine)
Cherry tomatoes
Basil, fresh leaves
Olive oil
Balsamic vinegar
Freshly ground black pepper

The bamboo skewers should be about 6 inches long. If you can't find a smaller size, you can always cut them. Drain the fresh mozzarella balls onto a paper towel.

Skewer your ingredients like this:

Tomato

Basil leaf

Mozzarella ball

Tomato

Basil leaf

Mozzarella ball

Lay the skewers on a platter and drizzle them with olive oil and balsamic vinegar. Remember, drizzle, don't drown them. Then grind a little fresh black pepper over the top and serve.

Summer Vegetable Frittata

In Italian, frittata means something fried. This super fantastic egg dish is the perfect thing to whip up when you are hungry and don't have a lot of time to make something nutritious and satisfying. It's easy and you will usually have what you need on hand.

1 tablespoon butter

1 tablespoon olive oil

½ medium onion, chopped

4 ounces of mushrooms, sliced

1 bunch asparagus, trimmed and sliced at an angle into bite-size pieces (about 1 cup chopped)

8 eggs

½ teaspoon salt

¼ teaspoon pepper

About ½ cup chopped fresh basil leaves

1 cup grated Parmesan cheese

Chives for garnishing

Preheat oven to 375°F. Melt the butter in a large ovenproof skillet and then add the olive oil. When both are heated through, sauté the onion until soft. After a couple minutes, add the sliced mushrooms and continue sautéing until the mushrooms start to brown a little. Next, add the asparagus, sauté for a couple more minutes, and stir in the basil. Remove the skillet from heat.

In a mixing bowl, beat the eggs until foamy. Add the salt, pepper and grated cheese, give it a little stir and pour over the vegetables in the skillet. Place in the oven and bake for 15 minutes, until the eggs are set. Remove from the oven, allow to cool for a few minutes, then slice and serve. Serves 6.

Tuscan Tomato Basil Soup

What can you do with all those beautiful tomatoes and that fresh basil from the garden? How about making a delicious Italian-style Tuscan soup? In the process you will learn how to remove tomato skins to create a bowl of creamy soup that goes perfectly with grilled cheese sandwiches or crispy cheese toasts.

1 tablespoon olive oil

1 tablespoon butter

½ medium onion, chopped

2 cloves garlic, minced

5 cups peeled, cored and chopped tomatoes (about 3 pounds)

2 cups chicken or vegetable stock

1 teaspoon sea salt

¼ teaspoon pepper

½ cup chopped fresh basil leaves

1 cup half and half

Pour olive oil into a stockpot. Add the butter and begin heating. Add the onion and stir until soft. Stir in garlic and sauté a few minutes more. Next, add the tomatoes and the chicken stock and cook over medium heat for 15 minutes, stirring occasionally.

Remove the pot from the heat and stir in salt, pepper, basil leaves and half and half. Then carefully pour into the blender in small amounts, and puree until smooth. This recipe should serve 4 to 6 but in my house it only serves 3 because we all like it so much.

HOW TO BLANCH TOMATOES
It's easy to peel tomatoes. Drop them whole into boiling water, then into cold water. The skins will come right off.

Torta Di Ricotta
(Cheese Pie)

A delicious and easy-to-make dessert, this one pretty much pleases everyone. It's that good.

½ cup butter, softened

1 cup raw sugar

3 eggs

1 teaspoon vanilla extract

1 cup ricotta cheese

1 cup white whole-wheat flour

1 tablespoon baking powder

¼ teaspoon salt

**Zest of 1 lemon
   (about 1 teaspoon)**

Preheat oven to 375°F. Begin by greasing a 9-inch cake pan with butter, then dust with flour. In the bowl of an electric mixer, cream together the butter and the sugar until light and fluffy. Add the eggs, one at a time, beating after each addition.

Next, mix in the vanilla extract and the ricotta cheese and beat until creamy.

Add the flour, half at a time, while you continue to mix. Then add the baking powder, salt and finally the lemon zest. It's good to have your rubber scraper nearby so you can scrape down the sides of the bowl to make sure your batter is smooth.

Pour batter into the prepared cake pan. Smooth out the batter and bake in the oven for 35 to 40 minutes or until the knife comes out clean after you have inserted it. Serves 6.

Polpettine
(Tiny Vegetable Balls)

The first time I made these I was so pleased because they were different and so good. It's another great dish for vegetarians and even for people who love meatballs.

2 medium zucchini, sliced
   (approximately 1 cup)

1 tablespoon fresh basil, minced finely

1 tablespoon fresh oregano, minced finely

2 cloves garlic, minced

4 green onions, sliced thin

½ cup finely chopped red bell pepper

1 egg, beaten

1 cup whole-wheat breadcrumbs

½ cup grated Parmesan cheese

½ cup pine nuts

Flour for dusting

Olive oil for frying

Begin by steaming the zucchini for about 3 minutes. Then put the zucchini on a paper towel to remove any excess moisture. Then chop very finely and place in a mixing bowl. Stir in all the remaining ingredients and mix very well.

Put flour on a plate and take about a tablespoon of this mixture and form gently into a ball. Dust each ball with the flour and get ready to fry them in the olive oil.

In a heavy skillet, place about ¼ inch of olive oil and heat the oil until it starts to shimmer. Carefully place the balls in the oil using a slotted spoon. Turn them carefully as they start to brown so all sides are cooked (about 4 minutes) and remove them to a paper towel to drain. Serve hot. Serves 4 to 6.

Jamaica

Jamaican food is lively, like the
reggae music I love so much. Jamaica also
has unusual and delicious fruits like ackee and
custard apple that I have never seen anywhere else.

Jerk Chicken with Mango and Pineapple Salsa

In Jamaica they have an expression, "Jamaica, No Problem." And you won't have a problem making this easy and flavorful dish.

6 boneless chicken breast cutlets, pounded until thin (If you have never pounded a chicken breast before, it requires a special tool. I place the chicken in a sealed plastic bag in order to do this and to keep the raw chicken away from any countertops.)

MARINADE

¼ cup olive oil

Juice of two limes (about 3 tablespoons)

2 cloves of garlic, minced

3 tablespoons soy sauce

1½ teaspoons onion powder

½ teaspoon nutmeg

1 teaspoon allspice

2 tablespoons honey

MANGO/PINEAPPLE SALSA

1 ripe mango, peeled and diced

½ fresh pineapple, peeled and diced

⅓ cup red onion, finely chopped

2 tablespoons fresh cilantro, chopped

2 tablespoons fresh lime juice

Mix the marinade ingredients together in a bowl. Add the chicken and toss well. Cover and refrigerate for at least half an hour.

While the chicken is marinating, blend all the salsa ingredients in another bowl and set aside.

Using your tongs, transfer the marinated chicken to a heated grill or under your broiler and cook for about 6-8 minutes on each side until browned and cooked through.

Serve with your favorite rice and the mango/pineapple salsa. Serves 6.

Japan

Some of my absolute favorite foods
come from Japan, like sushi and ramen noodles.
Did you know that in Japan it's considered extra good
manners to slurp noodles in soup? The louder, the better.

Sunomono
(Cucumber Salad)

If you've ever been to a sushi bar or Japanese restaurant, you may have tried sunomono. It's the simplest of salads—light, refreshing and easy. It's great to serve alongside a piece of fish and some rice.

---

1 English cucumber or 2 medium Japanese or Persian cucumbers

¼ teaspoon salt

¼ cup rice vinegar

1 teaspoon raw sugar

¼ teaspoon tamari soy sauce

2 tablespoons toasted sesame seeds

Peel the cucumber and then slice it as thin as you can. Place the cucumber slices in a small bowl, sprinkle with the salt and then mix well with your hands. Let them stand for about 5 minutes and the cucumber slices will start to sweat. The idea is to get the excess water out of them. After 5 minutes, drain the cucumbers and get out as much of the water as you can.

In a separate small bowl, mix together the rice vinegar, sugar and soy sauce. When the sugar is dissolved, pour the mixture over the cucumber and serve with a sprinkling of sesame seeds on each portion. Serves 4 to 6.

Fresh Fish in Parchment

This recipe makes an easy yet elegant meal and is full of flavor. You can use your favorite fish. Halibut, cod, salmon, bass will all work.

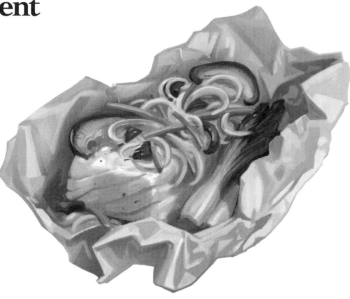

4 6-ounce fish fillets

4 ounces fresh sliced shiitake mushrooms

½ red bell pepper, sliced in thin strips

2 baby bok choy, thinly sliced

4 green onions, sliced

½ cup shredded carrots

FOR THE MARINADE

4 tablespoons mirin (sweet cooking sake)

1 tablespoon toasted sesame oil

Juice of 1 or 2 lemons

1 tablespoon fresh grated ginger

3 tablespoons tamari soy sauce

Coarse-grind black pepper

Preheat oven to 400°F. Begin by making the marinade. In a small bowl, whisk together the mirin, toasted sesame oil, lemon juice, ginger and soy sauce. Set aside while you make the packets.

Use pieces of parchment paper that are precut or about 15 inches square. I like to start with a piece of foil and place the parchment paper on top. Lay the paper out flat and then layer the vegetables in the middle: slices of mushroom, bell pepper, bok choy, green onion and shredded carrot. Next, lay the fish fillet on top, pour a portion of the marinade on top, sprinkle a little more onion on top and begin to fold the packets. The foil makes this easy to do and prevents the marinade from seeping out. Continue until you have used all the vegetables, fish and marinade.

Place the packets on a baking sheet and bake for 15 minutes. To serve, place packets on a plate and open carefully due to steam that may escape. Serves 4.

Lebanon

Lebanon is part of an area known as the
Cradle of Civilization, with many ancient ruins.
A meal there called mezze features as many as
one hundred different appetizers.

Baba Ghanouj

I first had this yummy dip when I was in Beirut, Lebanon. I didn't think I liked eggplant, but I loved this. Roasting the eggplant gives this dip a great smoky flavor.

1 large eggplant

2 tablespoons tahini (sesame butter)

2 tablespoons chopped parsley

2 cloves garlic, pressed

1 tablespoon olive oil

1 tablespoon lemon juice

1 teaspoon ground cumin

½ teaspoon paprika

½ teaspoon salt

Coarse-grind black pepper, to taste

First prick the eggplant with a fork, then place it directly under the broiler. Turn it slowly so that all sides are charred. When done the eggplant should be soft inside and the outside skin should be black.

Let the eggplant cool off before removing all the skin and cutting off the stem.

Place the eggplant in the jar of a blender or food processor. Add the remaining ingredients and blend until smooth. It should look like soft-serve ice cream. Place in a bowl and chill until ready to serve with fresh pita bread. Serves 4.

Tabouli

This salad is eaten all over the Middle East but some say it originated in Lebanon and Syria. It's made with bulghur, whole wheat that has been cooked, dried and cracked. That's why you don't need to cook it. It's just soaked in hot water. This is my favorite version.

2 cups fine (#1) bulghur

2 cups boiling water

½ cup thinly sliced green onions

1 medium onion, chopped very fine

1 bunch parsley, stems removed and chopped finely

1 bunch fresh mint leaves, chopped finely

2 large tomatoes, chopped very small, or 2 cups cherry tomatoes, quartered

> **DRESSING**
> ¼ cup extra virgin olive oil
> ¼ cup red wine vinegar
> Juice of 2 lemons
> 1 tablespoon tamari soy sauce
> Salt and pepper to taste

Place bulghur in a large mixing bowl. Cover with the boiling water and let stand for 5 to 10 minutes, then fluff the grains with a wooden spoon.

Add onions, parsley, mint and tomatoes and mix well.

Finally, add the dressing ingredients one at a time. Mix all ingredients thoroughly, chill in the refrigerator and toss once again before serving. Serves 6 to 8.

Mexico

Growing up in Arizona my family visited Mexico many times.
The north of Mexico is a desert with over seven hundred reptile species,
and the southern part is a tropical rainforest with jaguars and pumas.
I loved going there because everything is so different and
colorful, and the food remains some of my favorite.

Albondigas
(Meatball Soup)

This classic Mexican soup is crazy good, and with all of the dicing and chopping it can be a real family affair to prepare. I promise you it's worth the effort.

½ pound ground turkey

½ pound turkey sausage

1 egg, beaten

½ teaspoon garlic powder

½ cup cooked rice

¼ cup fresh mint leaves, finely chopped

½ cup cilantro, finely chopped

1 teaspoon ground cumin

1 teaspoon salt

½ teaspoon black pepper

6 cups chicken broth

½ medium onion, finely chopped

3 stalks celery, diced

1 cup cut green beans

2 medium carrots, diced

1 14-ounce can of petite-diced tomatoes

1 teaspoon ground cumin

2 teaspoons oregano

2 medium zucchini, sliced into rounds

1 teaspoon salt

½ teaspoon black pepper

Start by making the meatballs. In a large bowl mix together the ground turkey, turkey sausage, egg, garlic powder, rice, mint and cilantro leaves, cumin, salt and pepper. You can use a spoon or your clean hands to squish, mush and blend it all together.

Line a baking sheet or surface with wax paper. Make meatballs by taking about a tablespoon of the meat mixture and rolling balls between the palms of your hands. Place on the wax paper and then set aside. The mixture should make about 24 meatballs.

Next, put the chicken broth and all the veggies (except the zucchini) into a large stockpot. Stir in the can of tomatoes, cumin, oregano, salt and pepper and bring to a boil. Then lower the heat, cover with a lid and simmer for 15 minutes.

Using a spoon, gently drop the meatballs into the pot one at a time, being mindful not to splash the hot broth. Add the zucchini, cover the pot and simmer for 10 more minutes. Serves 8.

Red Snapper Veracruz

This is a great way to eat fish and the recipe is adaptable. If you can't find red snapper (also called rockfish) you can use tilapia or your favorite white fish.

2 pounds red snapper fillets

FOR THE FISH

3 tablespoons olive oil

Juice of 3 limes

Salt and pepper

FOR THE SAUCE

3 tablespoons olive oil

1 small red onion, chopped

2 cloves garlic

½ red, yellow or orange bell pepper, chopped

2 cups chopped cherry tomatoes cut in half (about 10 ounces)

1 teaspoon fresh oregano, chopped

½ cup chopped parsley

½ cup chopped green olives

1 teaspoon salt

¼ teaspoon pepper

Juice of 1 lemon

Preheat oven to 375°F. Lay the red snapper fillets in a baking dish and pour olive oil and lime juice over them. Then sprinkle with salt and pepper and marinate for half an hour. Place in the oven and bake for 15 to 20 minutes, or until fish is flaky all the way through.

While the fish is baking prepare the sauce to go over the fillets. Add the olive oil to a skillet and sauté the onion and garlic until soft. Then add the bell pepper and continue to sauté. Add the cherry tomatoes, oregano, parsley, olives and salt and pepper and continue to cook over medium heat for 5 minutes, stirring constantly. Finally, stir in the lemon juice.

Using a slotted spoon or a spatula, remove the fish fillets carefully onto a platter. There might be some liquid left in the baking dish but we won't be using that. Spoon the tomato/onion/olive mixture over the fillets and serve. Serves 4 to 6.

Enchiladas Suizas

Tomatillos are small fruits used to make green sauces in Mexico and many Latin American countries. They belong to the same family as tomatoes but they are light green and covered with a papery husk that must be removed before cooking.

1 dozen corn tortillas

2 cups grated Monterey Jack cheese

2 ears of cooked corn, kernels cut from the cob (about 2 cups)

½ cup plain Greek yogurt or sour cream

½ cup chopped cilantro

FOR TOMATILLO SAUCE

1 pound tomatillos, washed and quartered (make sure to cut out the tough core)

3 cloves garlic, chopped

1 onion, chopped

1 jalapeño chile, cut in half and seeds removed (optional)

1 cup chicken broth

1 tablespoon olive oil

Salt and pepper, to taste

½ cup chopped cilantro

Preheat oven to 375°F. Mix together the cheese, corn, yogurt and cilantro and set aside.

In a saucepan, add the tomatillos, garlic, onion, chile, chicken broth and olive oil, and bring to a boil. Lower the heat and simmer, covered, until the tomatillos and onion are tender, about 15 minutes.

Next, pour about 1 tablespoon of olive oil into a skillet and heat it. When hot, soften the tortillas by putting them into the skillet for a minute on each side. This is a good place to use your tongs. Fill each tortilla with a couple of tablespoons of the cheese and corn filling and then roll them. Stack them in a baking dish, pour the tomatillo sauce on top, and bake in the oven for about 30 minutes. The sauce should be bubbling up. Serve with a dollop of Greek yogurt or sour cream on each enchilada. Serves 6.

Morocco

Colorful and vibrant is how I would describe
Morocco. Africa's busiest city square, the Jemaa el-Fnaa,
is in the red city of Marrakech, where you can see musicians,
story tellers, magicians, dancers, and snake charmers, and
where, in the evening, food sellers set up stalls with
all kinds of delicious Moroccan delicacies.

Seven-Vegetable Tajine

This exotic dish from Morocco is prepared in a cone-shaped clay or ceramic cooking vessel called a tajine. You can use a Dutch oven if you don't have a tajine.

- 4 tablespoons olive oil
- 1 large onion, sliced thin
- 3 cloves garlic, minced
- ½ red or green bell pepper
- 2 teaspoons paprika
- 2 tablespoons cumin
- 1 tablespoon ras el hanout* (optional)
- 1 16-ounce can peeled tomatoes
- 3 carrots, peeled and cut lengthwise
- 1 pound new potatoes, cut in half

- 2 cups pumpkin, peeled and cut into chunks
- 1½ cups water or broth
- 2 cups zucchini, cut into chunks
- 1 can garbanzo beans, rinsed and drained
- 2 tablespoons tamari soy sauce
- 1 teaspoon salt
- ½ teaspoon freshly ground black pepper
- ½ cup chopped parsley
- ½ cup chopped cilantro
- 3 cups steamed whole-wheat couscous

*If you can't find this special Moroccan spice, use an extra tablespoon of cumin.

Heat the olive oil in your pot and add the onions. Sauté them until onions are soft, about 5 minutes.

Next, stir in the minced garlic and bell pepper and continue sautéing a few minutes more. Add the paprika, cumin and ras el hanout and stir in well for another minute.

Next, add the tomatoes and blend well. Then add the carrots, new potatoes, pumpkin and finally the water or broth. Bring mixture to a boil, then lower the flame to medium, cover and cook for 20 minutes.

Next, add the squash and garbanzo beans, tamari, salt and pepper. Cover with a lid and cook over medium heat for an additional 10 minutes. The vegetables should be tender but not mushy. Finally, stir in the chopped parsley and cilantro and serve over whole-wheat couscous. Serves 6 to 8.

Whole-Wheat Couscous

Couscous is an ancient grain product and is the traditional national dish of Morocco. It's actually made from semolina, so it's more like pasta. Nothing could be easier to prepare and it goes with so many dishes.

2 cups water
1 tablespoon butter
1 teaspoon salt
2 cups whole-wheat couscous

Combine water, butter and salt in a large saucepan and bring to a boil. Remove from the heat and pour the couscous into the saucepan. Stir well. Cover and let stand for 5 minutes. Fluff with a fork and you are ready to serve. Serves 6 to 8.

Mint Tea

Morocco's famous mint tea has become a symbol of their hospitality and culture, and is offered to guests as a welcoming gesture. They serve it several times a day in Morocco. You'll see why when you try it. It's smooth and minty.

2 to 3 teaspoons green tea leaves
4 cups boiling water
½ cup fresh mint leaves, washed
Raw sugar or honey

Place green tea leaves into a teapot. Pour boiling water into the pot and allow to steep for 1 minute. Pack the fresh mint leaves into the teapot and steep for a few minutes more. Add sugar or honey to taste.

Pour one glass of tea, then pour it back into the pot. (That's a little bit of tea magic for you to know when brewing fresh tea.)

To serve, pour tea into small glasses or cups. Serves 4 to 6.

Nigeria

There are over five hundred languages spoken
in this African country, though the national language is English.
No matter what language they speak, all agree about the importance
of the nutritionally rich yam in Nigerian culture, even honoring
the tuber vegetable at the New Yam Festival every August.

Efo Riro
(Vegan Spinach Stew)

Efo riro means stirred Nigerian spinach. This dish can also be made with Swiss chard or baby kale. Efo riro is popular in Nigeria so there are many versions of it. It's a perfect dish to serve over rice.

---

2 bunches of greens (spinach, chard or baby kale), washed and chopped

2 medium onions, chopped

2 red bell peppers, chopped

1 14-ounce can peeled Italian tomatoes

8 ounces mushrooms, sliced

⅓ cup olive oil

2 tablespoons curry powder

2 tablespoons tamari soy sauce

1 14-ounce can of garbanzo beans, drained

Begin by making a coarse puree in the blender or food processor. Use 1 chopped red bell pepper, 1 chopped onion and 1 14-ounce can of peeled tomatoes. Blend and put aside.

Next, add ⅓ cup olive oil to your skillet and sauté 1 chopped onion. When the onion starts to soften, add the chopped red bell pepper and continue to cook. Next, stir in the sliced mushrooms and sauté a few minutes longer.

Now stir in the puree and cook on medium heat for 3 or 4 minutes while you continue stirring. Blend in the curry powder and the soy sauce. Add the garbanzo beans and finally the spinach or greens. When the leaves wilt, your stew is done.

Note: Just like with the greens, you could add any beans in your pantry. I used tamari soy sauce to add umami to this dish because some ingredients used in Nigeria aren't readily available here. Serves 4 to 6.

Jollof Rice
(Chicken, Rice and Vegetable Dish)

This is a favorite dish in many West African countries. The name means "one pot" because it's all cooked in just one large pot. It's typically a very spicy dish so add the pepper afterwards for those who prefer less heat.

⅓ cup olive oil

2 large onions, sliced

3 or 4 cloves garlic, minced

1 28-ounce can stewed or diced tomatoes, with the juice

4 tablespoons tomato paste

1 teaspoon dried thyme

1 teaspoon dried or fresh rosemary

½ teaspoon grated nutmeg

½ teaspoon cayenne pepper

2 teaspoons salt

½ teaspoon black pepper

3 tablespoons Worcestershire sauce

1 whole chicken, cut into pieces (about 5 pounds)

2 cups water

1 cup basmati or quick-cook brown basmati rice

4 medium carrots, diced

1 pound green beans, trimmed and cut into 2-inch pieces

Pour olive oil into a large stockpot and heat. Add the onions and garlic and sauté at least 5 minutes, until soft, stirring constantly. Then add the tomatoes, tomato paste, Worcestershire sauce and all the spices and bring mixture to a boil.

Next, add the chicken pieces to the pot as well as the 2 cups of water, lower the heat to simmer, cover with a lid and cook for 30 minutes, stirring once or twice.

Now add the 1 cup of rice and the carrots and green beans. Give the pot a good stir, put the lid back on and continue to simmer for another 30 minutes. Serves 6 to 8.

Akwadu
(Baked Bananas)

Bananas are plentiful in West Africa, so this dessert is especially popular there. It's easy to prepare and is so delicious. It may become your new favorite way to enjoy a banana.

¼ cup melted butter
1 teaspoon grated lemon zest
3 tablespoons lemon juice
5 firm ripe bananas
5 tablespoons brown sugar

Preheat oven to 375°F. Pour melted butter into a baking dish (8-inch square). Add the lemon zest and lemon juice and blend. Peel the bananas and line them up in the baking dish, turning them over so all of the bananas are coated with the butter mixture. Sprinkle the brown sugar on top and place in the oven for 10 minutes. Using your mitts remove the pan and carefully turn over each banana. Then return the pan to the oven and bake for 10 minutes more. Serves 4 to 6.

Norway

Norway's food history dates back to the days of Vikings, when meals were stomach-busting feasts. And not very super natural. Today's Nordic way of eating is much healthier, with fresh berries, vegetables, light seafood, whole grains, nuts and seeds finding their way to the kitchen table more often than the heavy stews from centuries ago.

Salmon with Dill Sauce

The reason Norway is so famous for its salmon is because the country has a long coastline with cold waters that provide the perfect environment for year-round fishing. And you'll learn here that dill is a simple herb with a powerful punch.

2 pounds salmon fillets

2 tablespoons olive oil

1 teaspoon garlic powder

3 tablespoons lemon juice

1 cup plain Greek yogurt

2 tablespoons maple syrup

2 cloves fresh garlic, pressed

3 tablespoons chopped fresh dill

¼ teaspoon black pepper

½ teaspoon sea salt

Preheat oven to 400°F. Lightly oil a roasting dish or line a baking tray with foil and place the salmon fillets on, skin side down. Lightly drizzle the olive oil over the fish, then drizzle 2 tablespoons of the lemon juice, and finally sprinkle the fillets with garlic powder and salt and pepper. Roast the salmon in the oven until it's cooked through in the thickest part, about 15 minutes.

While the salmon is in the oven you can make the dill sauce. In a small bowl, whisk together the yogurt, 1 tablespoon of lemon juice, the garlic and maple syrup. Finally stir in the chopped fresh dill.

When the fish is cooked place on a serving plate, spoon the dill sauce over the top and add a sprig of dill for garnish. Delish! Serves 4.

Peru

There are over three thousand varieties of potatoes in Peru, where the Incas were the first to cultivate the now-essential food in countries across the globe. It's such an important part of the Peruvian culture that they have a potato day every May. And their bright purple potato is among the healthiest you can eat.

Quinoa Salad

Quinoa is popular because it's gluten-free and high in protein. It is really a seed but it is cooked like a grain and used in similar ways. It is also the food of the ancient Incas. If you visit Peru or a Peruvian restaurant you might come across a salad like this one.

1 cup quinoa

2 cups water, vegetable stock or chicken stock

1 medium or 2 small cucumbers, peeled and diced (about ½ cup)

½ cup red onion, finely chopped

½ cup red bell pepper, diced

1 cup cherry tomatoes, cut in half

½ cup fresh cilantro, chopped

½ cup parsley, finely chopped

½ cup red cabbage, finely chopped

6 ounces queso fresco or farmer's cheese, cubed

Juice of 2 limes, about ¼ cup

3 tablespoons olive oil

½ teaspoon salt

Prepare the quinoa first. Bring water or stock to a boil, stir in the quinoa, lower the heat to a simmer, cover with a lid and cook for 20 minutes, or until all the liquid has been absorbed. When done, give it a toss and place in a salad bowl to cool.

Next, chop all the ingredients (cucumber, red onion, bell pepper, cherry tomatoes, cilantro, red cabbage and cheese) and add to the quinoa. Stir in the lime juice, olive oil and salt, toss well and serve. Serves 4 to 6.

Ceviche

Ceviche is the national dish of Peru and can be served as an appetizer or a main dish. It is an ancient dish that was most likely eaten by the Incas. It looks fancy and tastes fantastic.

½ pound firm white fish (like sea bass, sole or snapper), cut into bite-sized pieces

Juice of 4 limes (about ½ cup)

1 cup thinly sliced cucumber (I like Persian or Japanese cucumbers for this)

1 cup sliced cherry tomatoes

3 tablespoons finely chopped red onion

3 tablespoons chopped cilantro

1 medium avocado, chopped

Salt and pepper

Blend all ingredients in a serving bowl and refrigerate, covered, for at least half an hour. The acid in the citrus juice "cooks" the fish, so it is not raw, but it is delicious.

At my home we like to eat the ceviche with some really good tortilla chips. It's great on a warm day. Serves 4 to 6.

Chicken with Aji Verde

This could be my favorite chicken. It's easy, it's fast and it has so much flavor. And the Aji Verde sauce is so good I want to put it on everything.

2 pounds boneless, skinless chicken thighs

FOR THE MARINADE
Juice of 2 limes

2 tablespoons olive oil

1 tablespoon honey

2 cloves garlic, pressed

2 teaspoons ground cumin

1 teaspoon oregano

1 teaspoon paprika

AJI VERDE SAUCE
½ cup Greek yogurt (plain)

2 cloves garlic, pressed

1 bunch cilantro, washed and stems trimmed

Juice of 1 lime

1 tablespoon honey

Salt and pepper to taste

A few drops hot sauce (for adventurous eaters)

In a small bowl, mix the marinade ingredients. Place the chicken thighs into a zipper-lock plastic bag, pour marinade over the chicken and squish it around. Then refrigerate for at least 1 hour.

To make the sauce, put all the ingredients into a blender and pulse until smooth.

Remove chicken, and grill or broil until slightly charred on both sides and cooked through, about 10 to 15 minutes. Serve with the Aji Verde sauce. Serves 4.

Poland

Poland is home to one of the oldest and largest salt mines in the world. It's no longer operational, but if you ever visit Krakow with your family it's an eye-opening experience to see how the salt we season our food with was mined over seven hundred years ago.

Potato Pancakes

Polish people love their potatoes and eat them many different ways. This is one of my favorite ways to enjoy a potato. And hold the maple syrup. These are savory, not sweet pancakes.

---

1 large egg, beaten

½ medium onion, grated

3 tablespoons whole-wheat or white whole-wheat flour

1 teaspoon salt

Black pepper to taste

Grapeseed oil for frying

Sour cream for garnish, if desired

Use a cheese grater to shred the potatoes. Put the shredded potatoes in a colander and rinse them in cold water, then drain them really well, squeezing out as much excess water as you can. I have used a clean tea cloth to do this. Then place potatoes in a medium-size bowl.

Next, stir in the beaten egg, grated onion, flour, salt and pepper and mix well.

Heat about ¼ inch of oil in a large nonstick skillet. Drop about ⅓ cup of potato mixture into the oil and flatten each pancake a little with your spatula. Fry both sides until they are golden brown and place on a paper towel. Serve immediately. They are great with a little sour cream on top. Makes 8 to 10 pancakes.

Scotland

The spiky purple thistle is the national flower of Scotland and is plentiful and edible. You can eat it like celery, make jelly or soups with it, or even prepare it as a super natural medicinal tea.

Rumbledethumps
(Potato and Cabbage Bake)

Rumbledethumps is a traditional dish from the Scottish Borders and very similar to a dish in England called Bubble and Squeak. It's fun to say out loud, fun to make and fun to eat.

---

2 pounds russet potatoes, peeled and cut into 2-inch chunks

6 tablespoons butter

½ cup milk

1 teaspoon salt

½ medium-size green cabbage, shredded (about 4 cups)

1 large brown onion, sliced thin

4 ounces cheddar cheese, grated

Preheat oven to 400°F. Place the potatoes into a large pot of water. Add 1 teaspoon of salt and bring to a boil. This will take about 15 minutes. You can test the potatoes to see if they are ready by carefully sticking a fork into them. They should break up a bit.

Drain the potatoes in a colander then return them to the pot. Add 3 tablespoons of the butter and the ½ cup milk, along with 1 teaspoon of salt and mash them using a potato masher. Try to make them smooth, though a few lumps won't matter. Set aside.

Melt the remaining 3 tablespoons of butter in a skillet and add the sliced onions. Sauté them until they wilt, then stir in the shredded cabbage and sauté for about 10 minutes until the cabbage is soft and has a bit of browning. Add salt and pepper to taste (about ½ teaspoon salt and ½ teaspoon black pepper). Add the onion/cabbage mixture to the mashed potatoes and mix well.

Put the potato/cabbage mixture into a 2-quart baking dish and top with the grated Cheddar cheese. Bake, uncovered, for 25 to 30 minutes until the top is browned. Besides having a great name, this dish will be loved by everyone in the family. Serves 4 to 6.

South Korea

World-famous for its kimchi, South Koreans
eat over 1.5 million tons of the salted and fermented
vegetables every year. It's so popular that some homes
even have special kimchi refrigerators.

Bibimbap
(Korean Rice Dish)

Bibimbap is the most well-known meal in Korea. The greatest thing about it is that you can really make it just about any way you like. It can be different every time and you don't need exact measurements. It's the perfect thing to make with leftover rice.

4 cups of cooked rice, any variety

Lettuce

Fresh vegetables like sliced mushrooms, grated carrots, radishes, shredded cabbage, and seaweed

Tofu, cubed

Pickled vegetables, like daikon

Black sesame seeds

Fried eggs

Chopped chicken or turkey or tuna

DRESSING
2 tablespoons toasted sesame oil

1 tablespoon tamari soy sauce

Juice of 1 lemon

2 tablespoons rice vinegar

1 teaspoon fresh grated ginger root

In a small bowl whisk together the dressing ingredients and set aside. Add 1 cup of rice to each of 4 individual serving bowls, then top with your favorite ingredients. Drizzle over the top of each bowl and serve. Serves 4.

Spain

Spain is home to siestas and fiestas, which means the Spanish like to take it easy after lunch and before dinner, and they like to party. Sounds good to me. Spain is also the world's largest olive oil producer and I don't think I could cook without extra virgin olive oil. The national dish is paella, a mixture of saffron rice, meat, seafood and vegetables.

Tapas-Style Toasted Almonds

In Spain, tapas means little appetizer plates. They can be pickled mushrooms, olives, little salads or toasted nuts. Almonds are one of the most common nuts served. When I lived on the island of Ibiza I loved seeing the almond trees in bloom. They looked like a sea of clouds. These are really fun to make and will transport you right under one of those beautiful almond trees.

2 cups raw almonds

1 tablespoon olive oil

¼ teaspoon sea salt

Preheat oven to 300°F. Begin by putting the almonds in a bowl, and pour boiling water over them. Let them stand for about 5 minutes and pour them into a colander to drain. Put them back in the bowl and cover with cold water for just a minute and drain well.

Here's the fun part. The skin will be loose and will just pop right off when you squeeze the almonds. Once the skins are off, dry the almonds well on paper towels. Put the skinned almonds back in the bowl and add the olive oil and sea salt. Mix with your hands until the almonds are evenly coated.

Next, spread the almonds out on a baking sheet and place in the oven for 20 minutes, or until just light golden brown. Halfway through the toasting, use a spatula to turn the almonds over so they roast evenly. Allow them to cool and then start munching.

Flan

Flan is the most popular dessert in Spain and in many Latin American countries. This recipe only has five ingredients and is simple to make. However, there is one tricky part, which is melting and caramelizing the sugar. It's amazing to see solid sugar become liquid. It's also very hot at that stage and can cause some bad burns, so be careful.

1 cup raw sugar

4 eggs

1 12-ounce can evaporated milk

1 teaspoon vanilla extract

¼ teaspoon cinnamon

Preheat oven to 325°F. Pour the sugar into a small saucepan and melt over medium heat. It helps to stir it quite a bit. When the sugar begins to melt and changes color, pour it into the bottom of six 3-inch ramekins.

In a medium-size bowl or in the jar of your electric blender, beat the eggs until they are fluffy. Add the milk, the rest of the sugar, vanilla and cinnamon. Pour this mixture into the ramekins.

Place the ramekins into a shallow baking pan filled with water. The water should come halfway up the sides. Carefully place the pan in the oven and bake for 45 to 50 minutes, when your testing knife should come out clean. Allow to cool. Then remove from water and chill in the refrigerator.

When you are ready to serve your flan, run a knife around the edge of each ramekin and turn upside down onto a small plate or bowl. Serves 6.

Gazpacho
(Cold Tomato Soup)

Every region in Spain has its own version of gazpacho. This one is from Andalusia and is my favorite. Eating it is like slurping your salad.

4 large ripe tomatoes, peeled, cored and chopped*

1 green bell pepper, cored, seeded and quartered

1 large cucumber, peeled and cut into cubes

1 medium onion, chopped

1 clove garlic, pressed

3 cups tomato juice

¼ cup olive oil

⅓ cup red wine vinegar

½ teaspoon salt

¼ teaspoon black pepper

Whole-wheat croutons

Get all your ingredients ready before you start. Put the tomatoes, cucumber, onion and garlic in the container of a food processor or the jar of an electric blender. (You will probably have to blend half of the ingredients at a time.) Blend until smooth.

Now add the tomato juice and blend again. Pour the mixture into a large bowl and add the olive oil, vinegar, salt and pepper. Refrigerate for 1 hour and then serve sprinkled with croutons. Serves 6 to 8.

* It's important to remove the skin of the tomatoes so the soup will be smooth.

Sweden

Thanks to a famous build-it-yourself furniture store,
you probably know all about Swedish meatballs and may have
sampled them yourself. But did you know that Sweden has a dedicated
day for eating candy? Called Saturday Sweets, it's a tradition that
dates back over sixty years and encourages tooth health
by only allowing sugary treats once a week.

Pannkaka
(Pancakes)

Pannkaka is one of the oldest recipes in this book, dating back to the early 1400s. These pancakes are like French crepes but they have more eggs, giving them extra protein, so they are great for breakfast.

1 cup milk

4 eggs

1 cup whole-wheat pastry flour or white whole-wheat flour

½ teaspoon salt

6 teaspoons butter for cooking

Place the milk, eggs, flour and salt into a blender and blend until smooth. Using the blender makes this so easy, though they can be whisked in a bowl if you prefer.

Melt 1 teaspoon of the butter in a nonstick skillet. When hot (but not burned) pour ½ cup of the batter into the skillet and swirl around until the entire bottom of the skillet is coated. Using a spatula, peek under the pancake and when it starts to turn golden, flip the pancake and cook until the other side is golden. Continue like this until you have made about 6 pancakes.

They can be topped with your favorite fruit jam, honey or maple syrup.

Taiwan

The national snack food of Taiwan is stinky tofu,
a fermented bean curd so strong that you may have to
pinch your nose just to sample a bite. Most Taiwanese
purchase it to enjoy as street food, since it's
just too stinky to make at home.

Danbing
(Egg Pancake)

These savory breakfast pancakes are a popular street food in Taiwan. This is a super easy way to make them and it's a quick and hot breakfast option you can eat on the go.

---

1 egg, beaten

1 green onion, thinly sliced

¼ teaspoon salt

A pinch of pepper, black or white

1 flour tortilla (approximately 10-inch size)

1 to 2 teaspoons vegetable oil

Add the sliced green onions, salt and pepper to the beaten egg. I like to mix them in a measuring cup so they are easy to pour. Heat the oil in a nonstick skillet. Then pour in the egg mixture, swirling around to cover the bottom of the skillet, like you were making a crepe or an omelet. Before the egg can cook, quickly place the flour tortilla on top and press gently with your spatula. Cook for a minute on medium heat.

Now, using your spatula, turn the whole pancake over and with some luck the tortilla will be stuck to the egg. Use your spatula to fold in both sides of the pancake. Cook for half a minute until both sides are golden brown. Serve hot. Serves 1.

Thailand

Thailand invented jasmine rice (also known as
"fragrant rice"), a staple at most Thai meals. Thai food is also
known for its fresh vegetables, bold spices, and use of peanuts and
coconuts. With a tendency toward dishes that are a harmonious blend of
salt, sweet, sour, spicy and even bitter ingredients, it's no wonder
Thai people are known for their happy smiles.

Mushroom and Tofu Laksa with Noodles

This noodle soup is popular throughout Southeast Asia. It is normally quite spicy but I will leave the spice up to your taste buds.

4 cups vegetable stock

1 14-ounce can coconut milk (about 1¾ cup)

2 tablespoons tomato paste

6 ounces shiitake mushrooms, with stalks removed and sliced thin

6 ounces firm tofu, drained and cut into cubes

1 cup shredded green cabbage

6 ounces chow mein noodles (If you can't find chow mein noodles, you can always use the same amount of angel hair pasta)

FOR SPICE PASTE:

1 jalapeño pepper, seeds removed and chopped

1 ½-inch piece of fresh ginger root, peeled and chopped

3 garlic cloves, minced

½ cup cilantro leaves, large stems removed

3 tablespoons vegetable oil

Juice of 1 lime

Puree these ingredients together to make a paste. Pulse the paste a few times until smooth. Put this paste into a stockpot, and over medium heat, fry the paste for a few minutes.

Next stir in the vegetable stock. Then add the coconut milk and bring to a boil. Stir in the tomato paste and when blended, add the mushrooms, the tofu, and the cabbage. Simmer for about 5 minutes.

Meanwhile, cook the noodles according to the package directions. When done add the noodles to each bowl and pour the broth over the noodles and serve with a sprig of cilantro on each. Serves 4 to 6.

Chicken Meatballs with Peanut Curry Sauce

I have also made this particular dish with red curry paste and it is equally fantastic.

1 pound ground chicken

½ cup breadcrumbs

1 egg, beaten

1 tablespoon tamari soy sauce

½ cup chopped onion

½ cup grated zucchini

½ teaspoon Chinese Five-Spice powder

½ teaspoon salt

¼ teaspoon black pepper

Fresh chopped cilantro for garnish

PEANUT CURRY SAUCE

1 cup coconut milk

1 tablespoon green curry paste

⅓ cup natural peanut butter

Juice of 1 lime

1 tablespoon tamari soy sauce

Preheat oven to 375°F. Blend all ingredients together in a large mixing bowl and mix well. Using your hands, form mixture into 12 golfball-sized meatballs. Place meatballs in a greased baking dish and bake for 20 to 25 minutes, until cooked through.

While the meatballs are baking, make the peanut curry sauce. Pour the coconut milk into a small saucepan. Whisk in the green curry paste, then the peanut butter, until mixture is smooth. Simmer over a low flame until mixture starts to thicken. Add the lime juice and tamari. Pour over the cooked meatballs and top with chopped cilantro. Serves 4 to 6.

Tibet

Tibet is considered one of the most secluded regions on Earth, known as the Roof of the World, and is surrounded by the world's two highest mountains, Mount Everest and K2. Since not much grows there, their most important crop is barley milled into tsampa, the staple food. The national beverage is hot buttered tea.

Shogog Khatsa
(Potato Curry)

A favorite at Tibetan picnics and gatherings, this vegetarian dish is best served with whole-wheat flatbread.

2 pounds russet potatoes, peeled and cut into chunks

1 teaspoon salt

¼ cup olive or peanut oil

1 large onion, chopped

3 cloves garlic, minced

1 large tomato, chopped

1 tablespoon fresh grated ginger

1 teaspoon turmeric

1 teaspoon paprika

1 teaspoon cumin

Salt and pepper

Cilantro, for garnish

Put the potatoes in a medium-sized pot and cover with cold water. Add 1 teaspoon of salt. Bring to a boil, then cook until fork-tender, about 15 minutes. Drain the potatoes into a colander and set aside.

Heat the olive or peanut oil in a skillet then sauté the onion until soft, then add the garlic and continue cooking. Next, add the tomato, lower the flame and cook for a few minutes more, until a sauce forms. Stir in the ginger, turmeric, paprika and cumin until well blended. Put the potatoes into a bowl. Add the onion/tomato mixture and mix well. Season to taste with salt and pepper and add chopped cilantro for a garnish. Serves 4 to 6.

Ukraine

The second largest country on the European continent,
Ukraine is also known as the "Bread Basket of Europe" thanks to
its significant grain contribution. Bread is so important in Ukraine
that people give a loaf of bread to welcome a new baby
or congratulate a family on a new home.

Beet Borscht

Borscht is a traditional food of Ukraine. The beets give it that beautiful ruby color, and here's a super natural tip: It's always the most colorful vegetables that have the most nutrition.

2 tablespoons butter

1 onion, chopped

1½ cups finely shredded cabbage

6 medium-size beets, peeled and grated

2 cups fresh or canned diced tomatoes

1 tablespoon red wine vinegar

1 teaspoon raw sugar

5 cups chicken or vegetable broth

1 cup sour cream or plain Greek yogurt

Fresh dill sprigs for garnish

Salt and pepper to taste

Melt the butter in a large stockpot and sauté the onions until they are soft. Next stir in the cabbage and the grated beets and sauté a few minutes longer. Then add the tomatoes, vinegar, sugar and broth.

Lower the heat to simmer, cover and cook for about 30 minutes.

Finally add salt and pepper. (Some chicken and vegetable broths already contain salt, so it's best to taste before you add.)

Serve this soup topped with a dollop of the sour cream or yogurt and a sprig of fresh dill. Serves 4 to 6.

SUPER NATURAL FAMILY COOKBOOK

United States

The hamburger was invented in the United States
and many consider it the country's national dish. In addition
to the traditional beef variety, super natural eaters can dig into
many healthy versions of burgers, including chickpea, turkey,
mushroom, black bean, crispy quinoa and even beet.

Cheesy Grits

If you travel anywhere in the southern
United States, you will find grits on the
menu, especially at breakfast time. Grits are
made from corn and usually eaten along
with eggs, bacon and biscuits. These
cheesy grits are good anytime.

---

2 cups milk

2 cups water

¼ teaspoon salt

1 cup stone-ground grits

2 tablespoons butter

**4 ounces sharp cheddar cheese,
   grated (about 2 cups)**

Pour milk, water and salt into a heavy
saucepan and bring to a boil. Stir in
the grits slowly and lower the heat
to simmer. Cook for about 5 minutes,
stirring occasionally to prevent lumps
from forming.

When the mixture is thick and creamy, remove
from the heat and add the butter and cheese. Stir
until well blended and serve immediately.
Serves 4 to 6.

Turkey Taco Salad

This salad is a meal in a bowl. The only thing it might need is some good cornbread on the side.

4 tablespoons olive oil

1 medium onion, chopped

1¼ pounds ground turkey

2 teaspoons natural mild taco seasoning

¾ cup mild salsa

½ teaspoon salt

1 head of romaine lettuce, shredded

1 cup diced jicama

1 cup shredded red cabbage

½ cup chopped cilantro

1 avocado, sliced

1 large carrot, grated

1 cup grated cheddar cheese

½ cup roasted pepitas (pumpkin seeds)

Organic blue corn chips

DRESSING

3 tablespoons olive oil

2 tablespoons rice vinegar

Juice of 2 limes

Pour olive oil into a skillet and heat the oil. Add the onion and sauté until soft, about 4 or 5 minutes. Then add in the turkey meat and break it up with a wooden spoon. Stir in the taco seasoning and the salsa and cook for about 10 minutes over medium heat, stirring often. Season with the salt and then let the mixture cool.

Next, put all the salad ingredients (lettuce, jicama, red cabbage, cilantro, avocado, carrot) into a salad bowl.

In a small bowl, use a whisk to blend the dressing ingredients. Pour dressing over the salad and toss. Put a scoop of turkey mixture on top of the salad, sprinkle with the grated cheese and pepitas, and garnish with the corn chips. Dig in. Serves 6 to 8.

Cowboy Beans

Head to the Wild West where these baked beans with a Southwestern twist were often enjoyed around a campfire. You can create that same flavor by using a Dutch oven on your stove.

2 cups dry pinto beans

2 tablespoons olive oil

8 ounces turkey bacon, diced

1 large onion, chopped

2 cloves garlic, minced

5 cups water

4 tablespoons molasses

½ cup tomato sauce

½ cup barbecue sauce

½ teaspoon salt

Begin by washing the beans. (Always wash dry beans before cooking them by putting them into the pot, covering with water, and giving them a good rinse before draining them.) Then cover the beans with water and soak them overnight.

Drain the beans into a colander and set aside for the moment. Heat the olive oil in the Dutch oven or heavy stockpot and add the chopped bacon. Fry the bacon in the oil for a few minutes, stirring constantly, until crispy. Then stir in the onion and sauté for 3 or 4 minutes. Add the garlic and continue sautéing for another minute. Add the drained beans and 5 cups of water and bring to a boil.

Lower the heat, cover the pot and simmer for 45 to 50 minutes or until the beans are tender.

Next, stir in the molasses, tomato sauce, barbecue sauce and salt. Raise the heat to medium and cook for an additional 20 minutes, stirring occasionally, until the sauce in the beans thickens. Serves 6 to 8.

Tex-Mex Casserole

I grew up living close to the border of Mexico, so my family had Mexican food often. I love the flavors of Mexican food so much I came up with this recipe, which is super easy to make and the perfect thing to serve at a party or take to a potluck.

---

2 tablespoons olive oil

1 onion, chopped

2 cups tomato sauce

1 tablespoon ground cumin

¼ teaspoon garlic powder

¼ teaspoon salt

6 corn tortillas

2 cups cooked brown rice

1 15-ounce can corn kernels (approximately 1½ cups fresh)

1 15-ounce can black beans

2 cups grated sharp cheddar cheese

Chopped fresh cilantro

Preheat oven to 375°F. Heat olive oil in a saucepan. Add the chopped onion and sauté until soft, a few minutes. Now add the tomato sauce. Stir in the cumin, garlic powder and salt and remove from stove.

Spread enough sauce to cover the bottom of a baking dish (about 12 x 8 inches). Then start the layering: 3 corn tortillas, brown rice, corn, black beans, half of the tomato sauce, half of the cheddar cheese, 3 more corn tortillas, all the rest of the sauce, then the rest of the cheese.

Pop the casserole into the oven and bake for 30 minutes until it starts to bubble. Remove from the oven and sprinkle with the cilantro. Let it stand for 10 minutes before serving. Serves 6.

Sloppy Joe Sliders

Sloppy Joes have been around quite a while and they have recently found new popularity served as sliders. Same taste, but smaller versions. I decided to see what would happen if I made Sloppy Joes with turkey and put them on small toasted buns. They are not only cute but super tasty too.

---

4 tablespoons olive oil

1 medium onion, chopped fine

½ red bell pepper, chopped fine

1 stalk celery, chopped fine

1¼ pounds ground turkey

1 tablespoon Worcestershire sauce

½ teaspoon garlic powder

½ cup organic tomato ketchup

½ cup tomato sauce

Salt (taste for salt since you might not need any)

Whole-wheat slider buns

Pour olive oil into a saucepan and add the onion. Sauté until soft, a few minutes, then add the red bell pepper and celery and continue sautéing. Next, add the turkey and cook for several minutes more, stirring constantly. Add the remaining ingredients, lower the heat and simmer for 15 minutes.

Toast the buns and add a generous amount of Sloppy Joe mixture on top of each bun and serve. Serves 6.

Persimmon Pudding

Like English "pudding," this is really more like a moist cake. Make sure you use the Hachiya variety for this recipe. It's a taller variety and its texture is nearly jelly-like when ripe.

---

2 cups persimmon pulp (about 3 persimmons, all skin removed)

4 eggs, beaten

½ cup butter, melted

¾ cup milk

½ cup raw sugar

1 teaspoon vanilla extract

1½ cups white whole-wheat flour

1 teaspoon baking powder

1 teaspoon baking soda

½ teaspoon salt

2 teaspoons cinnamon

½ teaspoon nutmeg

1 teaspoon ground ginger

1 cup chopped walnuts

Whipping cream

Preheat oven to 375°F. In a large bowl, mix the persimmon pulp, eggs, melted butter, milk, sugar and vanilla. Blend until smooth.

In a separate bowl mix the flour, baking powder, baking soda, salt and spices. Add the dry ingredients to the wet ingredients a little at a time, mixing well after each addition. Then stir in the chopped walnuts. Pour batter into a buttered 8-inch square baking pan and bake for 45 to 50 minutes. The pudding will rise like a cake and then fall when it cools.

Serve with a dollop of whipped cream. It may be eaten warm or cold. Serves 8.

venezuela

Home to the world's highest waterfall, tropical
jungles, anteaters and jaguars, this South American country
also happens to be where you can find some of the finest chocolate
in the world. Their famous hot chocolate is on the spicier
side of things thanks to the addition of star anise.

Besitos De Coco

A traditional Venezuelan recipe that is passed from generation to generation, it's a coconut macaroon that can even be dipped in chocolate for variety.

3 cups shredded sweetened coconut

4 tablespoons butter, softened

4 egg yolks

8 tablespoons flour

½ teaspoon salt

1 teaspoon vanilla extract

1 cup brown sugar, packed

Preheat oven to 350°F. Oil or spray a 19 x 9 x 2-inch glass baking dish and set aside.

Blend the butter and egg yolks together in a mixing bowl until smooth and creamy. Then slowly add the flour, salt, vanilla extract and brown sugar.

When the mixture is well blended, stir in the coconut. Use a teaspoon to scoop up the mixture and form it into ping-pong-sized balls. Line them up in your baking dish (about 20).

Put in the oven and bake for 35 to 40 minutes until they are golden brown all around. Remove from the oven and allow them to cool.

Vietnam

Vietnamese cuisine is considered one of the
healthiest in the world thanks to its minimal use of oil
and dairy, and focus on light, fresh, flavorful herbs to season
vegetable-heavy dishes. The food is so healthy that even their
most popular dessert, a mung bean soup, is super natural.

Banh Mi Wrap with Peanut Coconut Dressing

In Vietnam this street sandwich is served on a baguette-like roll and filled with meat. This is my healthier version, served on a whole-grain flour tortilla with the same great flavors.

PEANUT COCONUT DRESSING

½ cup all-natural crunchy salted peanut butter

½ cup coconut milk

Juice of 1 lime

1 teaspoon fresh grated ginger root

1 teaspoon rice vinegar

1 tablespoon brown sugar

1 tablespoon soy sauce

Add all the above ingredients (peanut butter, coconut milk, lime juice, ginger, rice vinegar, brown sugar and soy sauce) to a small saucepan and stir until smooth. Then cook over medium heat, stirring almost constantly for 4 to 5 minutes until the sauce is thick and creamy. Remove from the heat and allow the mixture to cool. Any leftover dressing must be refrigerated for future use.

FOR THE WRAP

Whole-grain flour tortillas, at least 10-inch size

Romaine lettuce leaves

Shredded carrot

Cilantro

Baked, marinated tofu

Bean sprouts

Begin by spreading a generous amount of the dressing on the tortilla or wrap. Then start layering slices of tofu, lettuce, shredded carrot, cilantro leaves and bean sprouts along the center of the wrap. Fold the ends in and roll up.

Ga Pho
(Chicken Noodle Soup)

This recipe has everything you could wish for in a soup—rich broth, chunks of chicken, rice noodles, fresh herbs, bean sprouts and lime juice. I love it year-round.

1 split chicken breast with bone and skin

3 cups water

3 cups chicken broth

2 shallots

1 inch ginger root

3 garlic cloves, whole

½ teaspoon fennel seeds

4 star anise

3 tablespoons fish sauce

Rice noodles (about 8 ounces)

Fresh cilantro

3 or 4 limes

Mung bean sprouts (about 1 cup)

Hoisin sauce

Place broth and water in a large soup pot. Add the chicken breast, cover and cook over medium heat for 30 minutes. Remove the chicken to a plate and allow to cool. Then cover the chicken and put it in the fridge for the moment.

Add the shallots, ginger root, garlic, fennel seeds, star anise and fish sauce to the broth. Cover the pot and simmer for 1 hour. Carefully strain the broth into a smaller pot. Remove the chicken from the refrigerator. Remove the skin and bones and pull the chicken apart with your clean fingers. Put shredded chunks of the chicken into the finished broth.

Next, bring a big pot of water to a boil, and then turn it off. Soak the noodles in the hot water for 10 minutes. Drain the noodles into a colander.

To serve this soup, put a pile of noodles into each bowl, then pour the chicken and broth over them. Add the cilantro, bean sprouts, wedges of lime and, if you like, stir in some hoisin sauce. Serves 6.

SUPER NATURAL FAMILY COOKBOOK